I0006721

Knowledge
CAPITAL
in the
Digital Society

C. Peter Waegemann

© C. Peter Waegemann 2012

ISBN-13: 978-1468016833

ISBN-10: 1468016830

Library of Congress: 2011962097

Keywords: apps, artificial intelligence, belief systems, brain-centric, business intelligence, capital, cloud, cloud computing, communication, consciousness, cyber warfare, cybercrime, cyberspace, data, data capture, digital communication, digital companion, digital hygiene, digital indexing, digital literacy, digital society, digital transparency, ebooks, electronic banking, emagazines, email, emotional motivators, emotions, enewspapers, enterprise intelligence, epublishing, GPS, human software, informatics, information, information capture, information disorder, information processing, information society, information technology, intelligence, internet, knowledge, knowledge capital, knowledge capital management, knowledge disorder, knowledge inventory, knowledge worker, learned motivators, life motivators, memory, mobile apps, mobile devices, motivators, net navigation, network, network-centric, network literacy, online, online banking, online education, online shopping, privacy, robots, security, smartphone, social media, social networks, supercommunity, systems-centric, technology, transparency, virtual, virtual activities, virtual community, virtual games, virtual world, web, WIC, WIC-centric, WIC dysfunctionality, WIC intelligence, WIC literacy, wisdom, world information community

Contents

Illustrations

Acknowledgments

I thank my life partner, Claudia Tessier, for her immense editing efforts and for guiding me regarding this book. Also, I am grateful to my son, Marc Waegemann, for his thoughtful comments and editorial suggestions.

Introduction

Over 400 million people go to Wikipedia every month to look up something.[1] More than two billion people are connected to the internet, which functions as a new, global virtual library. Half of the American population routinely communicates with virtual acquaintances and others using online services: they research, send email and text messages, get news, buy products, watch videos, make payments, rate restaurants, listen to music, play games, make travel reservations, read digital books, visit government websites, use personal apps on their mobile devices, and more. While some people marvel at these new opportunities, others fear the effect these new systems might have on intellectual capabilities.

We need to examine the role of information and knowledge in our lives. Think of children of the twentieth century (and before) who were drilled to learn by rote. Today, much of the information they memorized can be accessed on the internet, making the smartest child the one who can navigate information resources and connect the dots—that is, the one who understands the meaning and context of information. The need to learn by memorizing is now replaced by the need to thrive in the digital world: to be creative, to research, to connect the dots, and to manage information and knowledge. We must take information and knowledge more seriously, as they are the most valuable assets of our lives. The knowledge we acquire and the way we use information and knowledge represent our knowledge capital. I will make the case

---

1   Noam Cohen, "When Knowledge is Written, Does It Still Count?" *The New York Times*, August 07, 2011.

that, in the twenty-first century, knowledge capital will be central to our lives.

The new challenge concerns how one acquires knowledge, manages information, distinguishes useful from trivial, separates truth from spin, navigates information resources, and identifies belief systems according to established values while remaining open to alternatives, and how one continues to improve knowledge over a lifetime. People and organizations will have to acquire and navigate available knowledge online in order to create value. This is a new concept. Creating value within a society can lead to new products, innovative systems, higher productivity, and the creation of wealth and success. A set of new tools is available to anyone with a digital connection (in some countries, it starts with a mobile phone) and a desire to identify what knowledge can and should be obtained. All it takes is the will to manage one's personal or corporate or organizational information and knowledge.

Not so long ago, much of existing knowledge was available only to the privileged few who had access to libraries or universities. Further, the prevailing opinion was that *Homo sapiens* was wise (because of education and books), and that other living beings, particularly animals, were "stupid" or "ignorant". In recent decades, research has shown that human communication is just one form of communication. Other creatures have different means of capturing and communicating information. As we learn how ants, bees, or microbes manage and exchange information, our image of the role of information in a society of mammals, insects, and other animals is evolving.

Dreams from past centuries described fantastic "thinking machines" (Descartes) or unimaginable access to a wealth of information for most people. Such fantasies have become reality. Expanding access to information through technology, particularly in the form of computers, the internet, and mobile devices, is bringing about drastic changes in our society, our lives, and our relationships. The movement toward an Information Age has been discussed for decades. Within just a few generations, the majority of people in developed countries has moved from physical labor (on farms, in factories, etc.) to information management via devices that offer both knowledge and guidance. Consider people working with computers in banks, offices, and many other environments. They act as the interface to computers that handle financial issues and administrative or professional functions. As automated systems are perfected, this human interface will be minimized. In turn, jobs will be lost and people will have to find new ways of creating value; that is, new work using digital systems. Already, a writer decides what to address in an article, and then the computer system helps with the research and writing. A researcher defines a research project, and the digital systems do the math and research. An engineer plans and designs a manufacturing process, and a combination of machines and computer devices builds it. A driver determines the destination, and the GPS system provides guidance to find the way. In all of these cases, humans do the creative design and planning, and machines do the work. These are examples of the evolving roles that people have. But what does it mean in practical terms?

How does the Information Age change not just our thinking and our work, but also our customs and habits, and in turn, our way of life? Does the information society improve lives, or does it widen the gap between developed and undeveloped regions? What does it mean for the majority of people to become knowledge workers?

As I address these questions, I will argue that information is the most undervalued commodity for living beings on this planet. Next to nourishment, oxygen, and energy, information enables living beings to survive, adapt, and advance. We need to understand how certain information made us human and how the current information revolution is changing our lives. The writing of documents and books increased the volume of information available. The knowledge recorded in them supported the brain, partly integrated into it through memory; it was also partly available in libraries and other resources that could supplement the brain's capacity. What was not memorized could be looked up in books and other documents. The brain and its extension, the mind, were the undisputed center of the human information system.

In the new information system, the roles of brain and external databases are shifting. The information stored on networks is much greater than the capacity of any brain to absorb and retain. At the turn of this century, when the internet was still in its infancy, a study by the University of California at Berkeley determined that the internet held about 37,000 libraries the size of the Library of Congress.[2] It is difficult to estimate how many thousands of times larger it has grown since. As more books are digitized and information is integrated into this new planetary knowledge base, the ratio between what the internet and what the brain can store has shifted dramatically. The sum of available digital information far surpasses the brain's capacity to retain; at the same time, the memory chip of today's computer keeps increasing in capacity and decreasing in size, while the capacity of the human brain has remained relatively static. The world's knowledge base is shifting from being brain-centric to systems-centric, with the brain no longer holding the central role. In this new, networked knowledge base, the brain's role will be different but still dominant. This requires changes in our information processing rules. Join me to explore what this does to our understanding of intelligence.

When one explores the path to human improvements through information processing and storage capabilities, an interesting pattern emerges. The first step led us away from primal intelligence that was focused on survival and reproduction. Theoretical thinking distinguished our ancestors' intelligence from that of the animal world. The second step was knowledge accumulation through writing and its distribution, eventually in the form of books. Then, knowledge led to societies based on production of goods: the production of food, then clothing, then so-called luxury goods. Thousands of years ago, domesticated animals and slaves supplied the necessary production energy; later, water, fire, and wind were

---

2   Peter Lyman and Hal R Varian, School of Information Management and Systems, University of California at Berkeley, "How Much Information? 2003." http://www2.sims.berkeley.edu/research/projects/how-much-info-2003/.

used. Then, the knowledge of industrial fossil fuel extraction and of creating electricity brought substantial increases in productivity.

The world of the nineteenth and twentieth centuries was about the use of "new" technologies. These enabled people to create the amenities of the modern world. Capitalism based on resources and increased productivity has governed, particularly since the fall of most communist countries. The search for greater productivity has led to increased use of automation. Machines equipped with computers can do the work of many people. Automation will continue to be more efficient and will take away jobs that were traditionally people's way of making a living. This book will explain the change from the productivity objective to information-based value creation.

Information may be the currency of the twenty-first century and beyond. For some time, governments have been operating secret services to collect and interpret the information of other competing entities. Now, corporations and organizations, large and small, need to develop systems that obtain information, direct responses to adverse public messages, identify and manage organizational knowledge, and govern the internal and external information flow. More than ever, leaked information may be the downfall of organizations, from businesses to governments, while some will excel and succeed because of information they obtain and exploit. Manipulating information is already common practice among media and political parties, but it will reach new, previously unthinkable dimensions (with attendant dangers). Advertising is moving from printed media to digital product targeting, changing long-established methods of information dissemination. All these developments taken together represent the beginning of a new paradigm through which the creation, management, representation, distortion, and validation of information will greatly affect our lives.

So, how is the *computer* changing our lives? And how is the *internet* changing our thinking? I will argue that an intertwined combination of elements, including computers and the internet, is changing social patterns, informational organization, economic principles, value definitions (such as freedom), information processing rules, and our intelligence. These changes are not only created by technologies, but also by a new phenomenon that affects people in both undeveloped and developed countries. The new system is a networked supercommunity that I call WIC (short for *world information community*, pronounced "wik"). WIC people have common access to an unimaginable wealth of knowledge, can network with people around the globe, and can receive services from organizations that may be thousands of miles away (e.g., online banking, telemedicine, and knowledge and instructions from mobile phones via satellites). Perhaps even more important and with greater consequences, WIC gives people a voice, i.e., the opportunity to express their opinions and to communicate information widely.

WIC is changing industries, particularly such information-intense fields as publishing, advertising, banking, medicine, and perhaps most of all, education. Not robots, but automation and digital companions are changing our lives. WIC offers tremendous opportunities, but it also brings threats that information will be misused—that the world will slip into a new form of Dark Ages if information is ever centrally manipulated, lost, or controlled. In addition, the future challenge to humans is to understand their (sometimes irrational, sometimes energizing and positive) emotional motivators and limit or erase any negative actions they cause, while accepting guidance toward logical and rational information processing. Explore with me a broad-brush description of human software, addressing such questions as: Will computer guidance help people understand and manage their emotional impulses and alert them to the potential consequences of decisions?

People have the option to follow overall ethical goals to make life on this planet better. Also, a new informational democracy is on the horizon, where subject matter expertise trumps traditional hierarchies of traditional knowledge. A citizen's camera-phone photo of an incident may be more convincing and reliable than a contradicting statement by an "authority." Think of encyclopedias being edited by millions of people from many countries instead of by a few editors. From the learned editors' point of view, this accumulated information looks like it comes from "know-nothings," but the wisdom of a crowd of subject matter experts matches and expands knowledge bases to a level that could not be achieved in the past.

My point is that we are at just the beginning of changes that can bring wonderful opportunities, but they also carry substantial threats. The new understanding of freedom will focus on transparency and information accessibility. But most of all, we must explore what it means, both at a personal level and an organizational level, to prepare for a new way of managing our knowledge and information. How we manage our knowledge capital will be one of the most important challenges of the next decades. People's identity, social rank, financial well-being, and intellectual status will be defined by their accumulation and utilization of knowledge. "You are what you know" will take on new meaning—that is, how you navigate the system, understand the context of information, manage your emotional motivators, and create value will define your role on this planet.

1

The New Frontier: WIC

We sense that information technologies are stimulating dramatic changes. Newspapers and magazines are replete with articles attempting to describe what is going on and how it affects us. Books explore how the internet is changing our thinking. People are trying to understand the full extent of these changes: some compare the changes brought by computers and the internet to the developments first stimulated by Gutenberg's creation of moveable type. In fact, the changes due to information technologies are now bigger and have a greater impact than anything that has come before. The range of information access, the extent of information processing power, and the opportunities for collaboration (via networks) are unprecedented. New ways of influencing communities are emerging, and behaviors are changing. Digital companions guide us to find shops, doctors, and restaurant recommendations; GPS systems are guiding us geographically; and many more developments are dramatically changing our lives.

Compare these changes with those of the late nineteenth and early twentieth centuries. For instance, the initial goal of replacing oil lamps when electricity became available expanded into other, previously unforeseeable applications. Few could anticipate how electricity would change lives beyond providing light. More than a hundred years later, people rarely marvel over the switch that brings air conditioning or heat, operates electrical machines, and enables entertainment experiences, communication over distance, extended food freshness, electric train travel, many safety, communication, and entertainment features in automobiles, and more. Who would have thought electricity would bring all this? Electricity was probably the discovery that most changed peoples' lives in the twentieth century, yet few understand its intricacies, and even fewer could have anticipated the extent of its impact. Only power outages make us aware of just how much we take for granted about flipping that switch.

The disruptive impact of digital technologies on people's lives as they bring new ways of communication, increase information-based work, and make instantly available huge amounts of information demonstrates the power of this revolution. These technologies enable people to live different lives from those they were used to. Think of online shopping, online research, virtual offices, data communication rather than voice, and so on. The combination of computing and communication power creates a new virtual information community without borders and with uncounted subcommunities, bridging continents and cultures, enabling information transfer to undeveloped and infrastructure-challenged countries, providing information to all people with access, and granting them voice.

Old patterns of close families, in which adult children supported their parents and family members shared and complemented one another, are diminishing. People move to different cities, states, and even countries that may be thousands of miles away. The old communities of village, town—even state and nation—are being called into question as people communicate more with their digital network friends than with their neighbors. Instead of going to local shops, people are buying directly online from a store that may be halfway around the globe. Similarly, knowledge is being obtained from faraway places rather than just from the local newspaper.

To understand how this is changing life on the whole planet, we must look beyond the effect that computers have on our lives and businesses, beyond how the internet is changing our thinking, and beyond how social media are changing businesses and relationships. Enabled by these new technologies, a new structure—a world information community (WIC)—is emerging. Being a part of WIC means taking advantage of new computing and communication systems to create new information communities and knowledge management opportunities. Further, there is a moral obligation to overcome the digital gap and address the needs of those who live in conditions that exclude them from WIC due to infrastructure, government, financial, or other reasons.

Knowledge Capital

More than 150 years ago, the exploitation of labor and the central role of money in societies were highlighted by Karl Marx and Friedrich Engels. Capitalism is based on money accumulation and management. "Money makes the world go round" is not only a popular cabaret theme, but also a subject of study and research. It is time to recognize that knowledge is also a currency for success and well-being. Knowledge accumulation and knowledge management are increasingly important in our societies. *Knowledge capital* is knowledge that an organization or individual has accumulated for success. When knowledge capital is managed properly, the health and success of a person or an organization can be improved and better sustained. Knowledge capital must be spent at the right time and in the right circumstances. The wealth of information available about each of us and the world is dramatically changing our daily lives, our relationships, and ourselves. Will the average person in the year 2040 have a complete history of not just her life, but also of her knowledge development? Will an employer request the data of all her formal education as well as a transcript of the books that she has read, all the news she has ever followed, how she manages her emotions, which political and religious beliefs she has, which websites she visits regularly, and so on? The dark side of stereotyping, personal transparency, and loss of privacy through technology is a real threat we must take seriously.

This could become a different "brave new world" from that suggested by Aldous Huxley. The information explosion offers many advantages, but it also poses many threats to the values we have cherished. The history of information processing and development suggests that there is no turning back the clock. The networked information world will continue to expand. It is important to recognize that information and knowledge are the most valuable assets of all living beings. They determine our well-being, our intelligence, our meaning, our roles in life, our competitive success, and our ability to maneuver within and between belief systems and society.

WIC Elements

WIC consists of at least the following six elements: Computers, software, the internet, indexing, mobile devices, and the cloud.

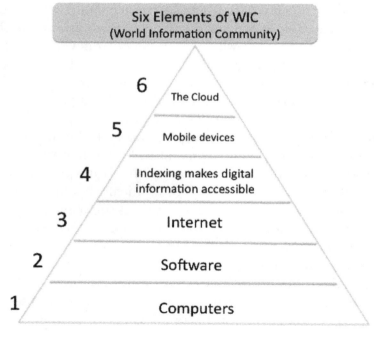

Figure 1. Six elements of WIC

1 THE PATH TO COMPUTERS

The computer can act as extended memory for the brain as well as a device that captures information and/or "thinks" for us. Mechanical devices to help the brain with computing functions were developed early in civilization, particularly in the mathematical information-processing field. If thinking processes are broken down into straightforward algorithms, then mathematical thinking can be most easily done by nonhumans (as with a calculator). In Asia nearly five thousand years ago, the abacus was developed as a mechanical aid for addition, subtraction, multiplication, division, square root, and cubic root functions. The Antikythera mechanism is the oldest known computing device; used for astronomical calculation, it has been dated back about 2100 years.[3] From the seventeenth century until the 1960s, the slide rule aided not only with multiplication and division functions, but also in computing roots, logarithms, and trigonometry. It is considered one of the first manual analog computing devices. Over time, a range of other analog devices helped people to calculate specific mathematical problems. In other words, given certain factors and appropriate algorithms, a device could relatively easily compute a specific mathematical problem by simulating the human thinking process.

The calculator's first mechanical models appeared in the seventeenth century and were further developed until they were integrated into modern computers. In addition to calculating, pre-computer devices were also used to run machines, such as textile looms. As with many technological developments, electricity had an impact on calculators. The step from the mechanical to the electric calculator led to more sophisticated devices. When they became portable, we could meet many more daily mathematical challenges, including those in educational environments and sophisticated professional situations. Teachers and many others became concerned that young people would decline in the ability to compute basic arithmetic in their heads and that future generations would lose it. In Hungary, students were reportedly not allowed to use portable calculators

---

3   Peter James and Nick Thorpe, *Ancient Inventions* (New York: Ballantine Books, 1995), 121.

so that their mental math capabilities would be better than those who did use them.[4] This concern disappeared when schools found that calculators do not diminish math capabilities; in fact, they allow students to shift to more conceptual thinking. In other words, humans have reached a stage where devices free the brain to use higher functionalities. In some ways, the calculator is analogous to a spell-checking application in word processing software that aids the writer with spelling and even grammar but cannot yet create an essay or distinguish between similar words by meaning or context. Similarly, integrated circuit chips in modern phones hold the memory function where a phone number is mapped to a name. This has led to the general trend toward not remembering phone numbers; the device stores them with contact names, so we no longer need be burdened with that task.

However, solving mathematical problems or mapping a number to a name is one thing; a machine that can do memory functions, process, index, store, and retrieve information to provide decision support is quite another. The step toward the binary approach, started several hundred years ago, enabled the creation of data processing machines. For some time, these were huge, number-crunching machines. Even today, the information technology department in some institutions continues to be called the "data processing" department. The next step was the all-purpose personal computer (PC) that could do increasingly complex "thinking" operations based on certain conditions that were programmed for specific actions. For instance, when programmed for word processing, software allows easy deleting, arranging, searching, and replacement functions coupled with grammar and spell-checking. Similarly, spreadsheet software offers options for arranging and manipulating data, as well as for displaying results.

Until the late 1970s, large databases where organizations kept information about people (customers, clients, members, residents, subscribers) or other things were recorded on cards stored in large cabinets. These cards were manually organized, searched, and updated. For many organizations, computer systems allowed many of these asset records to be more efficiently maintained in

---

4   Personal conversation in Budapest in 1974.

semi-digital format. They could be kept more current and used as official, even legal, records. Particularly with systems that record phone calls, organizations now have a more complete history of a customer's inquiry, including behavior regarding a specific issue.

The computer is an electrical-mechanical device that can process a number of programmed algorithms. Technology's greatest achievement is to allow more integrated circuits (ICs) to store information in less and less space to process a growing number of algorithms. Moore's law, the doubling of processing capability by doubling the number of transistors every twenty-four months, has been remarkably accurate in the more than fifty years since it was postulated, and this progression is expected to continue. It is difficult to grasp the importance of these developments, because never before has a technology grown in capability while shrinking in size, or at such an unprecedented rate. If information is the essence of life on this planet, then the integrated circuit is the enabler of this new frontier.

2 INSTRUCTIONS FOR INFORMATION PROCESSING TASKS: SOFTWARE

The second element of WIC consists of software: operating systems that govern basic operations and application software that governs the rules and processes for specific tasks. Computer hardware by itself cannot function without systems that give it specific instructions and operating rules. Operating systems are like preschool and elementary school for computers: they form a buildable base for developing higher skills and levels of intelligence. And, like languages, operating systems evolved as platforms for processing and exchanging data, information, and knowledge. Learning the proper use of a language includes how to use its rules and integrate appropriate vocabulary, the reigning intellectual challenge of the last several thousand years.

The new challenge with WIC is learning to manage computer software, and it will become a required skill. Software developments respond to hardware developments, from mainframe to minicomputers and PCs to client networks, mobile systems, and cloud computing. Early machine language programs consisted of long sequences of instructions written in binary code for adding, subtracting, and comparing data. The second generation of assembly languages was easier to use. In the 1980s, the first decades of personal computing were enabled by Microsoft and other operating systems that, in turn, prompted software application development. Since then, development has moved to more complex applications and to simpler, less costly applications for portable mobile devices. Apple's iPhone platform is an example of how thousands of developers can create functionality in an application (app). App development is the computer literacy of the future. As operating systems evolve to provide less complex ways to create application software, the average knowledge worker will be expected to write and amend specific apps. Strong indications of these developments can already be seen. In general, software that enables machine learning and uses artificial intelligence is currently in an embryonic stage, but it will have a huge impact as intelligence and production design enter a new age.

3 CONNECTING COMPUTERS AND DEVICES: THE INTERNET

The third element of WIC is the internet, the worldwide network of billions of interlinked computers. About twenty years ago, I described a dream to a group of information technology professionals: Wouldn't it be wonderful if all libraries of the world could be linked to allow anyone simultaneous access to any book or document and have it automatically translated? Just a few years later, this dream started to become reality. The internet even exceeds the dream of passive knowledge acquisition, as it enables information sharing and coordinated processing among computer systems and networks. Consider each computer a mechanical combination of information processing parts that are internally linked so that they function as a whole through their software. This connecting of internal parts increased computer power, and linking computers created powerful networks, but connecting all of these networks into a global system became a step unequalled in its importance.

Born out of government and academic research and design, the complex network of internet computers sharing their information and increasing their processing power is a historic step for humanity. Today an internet collapse would bring whole industries down. Predictions that the internet may not sustain growth and that it may break down demonstrate its critics' fears. They have been repeatedly proven wrong: the internet has grown beyond anyone's imagination and without the direct control of any authority. The network of internet service providers that cover the globe and manage all communication according to a suite of internet standards has been proven to work well. This internet, originally a vehicle to exchange messages, led to the stream of email that has increasingly replaced paper letters sent through the postal system. In a short time, it has changed how a majority of people in information societies communicate. In addition to email, chat, and direct communication through websites and other methods, digital, text-based communication has gained in volume and usage. The internet is causing the demise of national postal systems and has impacted bulk mail advertising as well as voice-based phone communication. It also enables connectivity to billions of websites. The web has become the central information display window of communication for any organization or individual. At the same time, developments are racing ahead toward community and social media-based features such as Twitter, Facebook, LinkedIn, and Google+.

4 MAKING SENSE OF HUNDREDS OF BILLIONS OF INFORMATION PIECES: INDEXING

The fourth WIC ingredient is the indexing of all information. In fact, connecting and indexing information created the basis for WIC. The amount of information stored and accessible on the worldwide information net would be unmanageable otherwise. About five hundred years ago, Descartes stated: "Even if all knowledge could be found in books, where it is mixed in with so many useless things and confusingly heaped in such volumes, it would take longer to read these books than we have to live in this life."[5] In many ways, this is still true today. Since large quantities of books were first collected, the challenge has been to find a particular document or specific information of interest easily and quickly. Thus, the key to knowledge is not the amassing of books and documents, but the creation of an information navigation system.

Future informatics specialists might describe the twenty-first century as the era of indexing. At first glance, commercially driven indexing breakthroughs, such as Google, Yahoo, AltaVista, Ask Jeeves, and Bing, appear to have solved the problem, because they are so much more developed than any previous parsing and indexing attempts. However, such services represent just the beginning of attempts to provide pathways to navigate all the public, corporate, organizational, and other libraries, as well as documents and information stored elsewhere. Along with the movement toward indexing the content of trillions of documents and other resources will come the goal to create a searchable synopsis of any article, book, or document. Imagine that any person might have access not only to any presentation ever given, any book or article ever written, any speech ever delivered, but also an indexed synopsis of each.

This possibility brings three major issues to the forefront. First, as noted above, people are overwhelmed by the abundance of information—they felt this way even in the relatively low-information past. Second is the question of value and truth. The web is not controlled by gatekeepers who check, validate, question, or reject what is proposed to be published there. So, the difficulty of identifying correct, incorrect, or misleading information has come to the fore. Third is the issue of internet indexing through frequency algorithms, which deliver to a user the most-requested information and most-visited sites. This process may be perceived as negative, because it gives preference to previously viewed information over new information and prioritizes a large organization's information over something potentially more valuable from a lesser-known entity. More sophisti-

---

5   Rene Descartes, *Meditations on First Philosophy* (Cambridge University Press, 1996), 10:497-8.

cated search engine alternatives may be based on advanced subject matter features, belief systems, and other semantic criteria.

The immense progress in indexing allows instant search engine answers to almost any general question: *How many time zones are in Russia? How long does it take to fly to the moon? What is the capital of Burkina Faso?* These databases are constantly updated. For example, GPS users alert a navigation system's designers that it does not always provide the shortest or best way to a destination because of small roads or obstacles it may not have included. These systems will improve as special information is included, such as bike paths (even distinguished into routes for mountain and city bikes). Similarly, the nature lover may see data on recent sightings of birds or wild animals while on a specific hike.

Thus, the planned digitizing and indexing of more than 100 million books and other documents marks the beginning of the twenty-first century as the era of knowledge. In many ways, indexing is about making sense of information that previously was only available in pieces to a selected few. Two fields that indexing has not yet greatly affected are medicine and law. Medicine still uses a variety of different systems for coding and terminology. A comprehensive medical nomenclature system would help clinicians, patients, and others, but it remains to be developed and adopted. For law, a complete legal case navigation system must include all cases, the reasoning behind each, and a semantic search system. These examples show that WIC has so far only begun the immense task of sorting and indexing all knowledge.

5 MOBILE DEVICES

The fifth ingredient of WIC is the mobile device that provides access to the four previous features, plus easy communication. Portable communication and computing devices are crowned with easy-to-produce and easy-to-follow apps. At the time of this writing, over six billion people subscribe to wireless phone access. Compare this to the fewer than one billion who own an automobile or a PC and the 1.5 billion who have a television set or a bank card. The introduction of mobile phones has been the fastest and most successful of any new technology.[6] The obvious advantage of mobile phones is that one is available for communication from anywhere and at any time.

The mobile phone has also quietly brought a remarkable alteration in the information field: the shift from transmitting voice to transmitting data. The text message has captured a generation in a way that many older people find difficult to understand. Text messages are often transmitted through telecommunications carriers (the companies that built the telephone infrastructure), not via the internet. They are a different type of expression from speaking on the phone or writing email. They can be more precise than other forms of communication, and they are usually shorter than traditional voice communications. Because the tone of speech can express moods and emotions that are not as easily communicated in text messages, it is now customary to attach emoticons to reflect mood, as well as to express some emotional content in words such as *haha, sooo, grrr,* and *hmm.* Inevitably, people claim that data communication lacks some of the richness in voice communication, while users find it more expressive and convenient as well as faster and simpler. Thus, data communication works for millions of young people who prefer it to voice.

More and more human communication will probably be in text or data form. Organizations are switching from telephone operators to systems where a user enters a message into a computer or smartphone through a dedicated website or mobile app. (Chapter 8 describes several.) Some readers may remember the old ways: calling a travel agent to explain travel plans; chatting with a bank teller to deposit a check; speaking with a store salesperson about a potential purchase; calling a doctor's office for an appointment; making reservations for hotels or restaurants by telephone; and so on. Many of these conversations are being replaced by the entry of concrete data into a smartphone app. When communicating in this manner, the person must provide specific and accurate information. The process also creates a precise record that can be used for clarification or in case of subsequent disputes. There is a choice:

---

6   C Peter Waegemann and Claudia Tessier, *The Impact of mHealth* (Boston, MA: mHealth Initiative, 2010).

email is discoverable and difficult to erase, but chat is generally not recorded and text messages are rarely retained.

Apps can guide people and change their behavior and lives, as well as inform and entertain them. Pictures and images can increasingly be incorporated in communication. They can be used as evidence where words do not suffice. A video or picture of unruly, inappropriate, or illegal behavior is the evidence of the future, and any person with a smartphone camera can record, circulate, or retain it. Individuals have never before had this kind of power to record evidence, be it in the workplace, on the street, or in a bar. Democracy has taken one major step forward in giving people a voice. Easy conditions for app development have stimulated a huge wave of apps to guide people personally and professionally.

6 THE CLOUD

The sixth WIC ingredient is the movement away from the power of the individual computer or device to cloud computing: a natural step in WIC development. Cloud computing is a system in which computation processes, software, data storage and retrieval, and other functions are hosted on a network of remote servers rather than on a local server or personal computer. They are specifically designed to store data in multiple safe places as well as to update and maintain systems, software, and computer services. Because these storage places are distributed throughout the world, they are called "the cloud."

To understand the move to the cloud, consider computer weaknesses. A single computer's digital information processing is vulnerable to crashes and other user problems (e.g., climate or power fluctuations, inappropriate or uninformed handling, etc.). Hardware will fail and must be upgraded. When an average user maintains both hardware and software, the likelihood of insufficient backup and security is enormous. It is easy for users to live in a dream world, in faith that the mechanics of the computer will not fail. Software needs constant upgrades and repair patches that pose a challenge for millions of people in varying locations. In contrast, internet connectivity is reliable. There is merit to the idea that WIC knowledge, at least in large part, should be stored in a distributed network of servers that has the highest likelihood for survival, even if power is not available due to local conditions or national tragedy. If one server fails, others can retrieve what is lost.

It is a natural step to move toward saving software and computer-stored information in a network of remote servers that can safeguard it better than the average user, that can upgrade and repair software better because it has central control, and that can safeguard information better against environmental, terrorist, or other attacks. The advantages of inexpensive devices connected to a remote network are manifold: lower purchase cost, easier maintenance, and higher efficiency. Instead of updating many individual computers, only the cloud system has to be updated. Compare the cloud to developments in supplying power to mills and factories. In the eighteenth and nineteenth centuries, production operations had to generate their own power. Mills were built on brooks and rivers to drive the equipment. Today, their power arrives through a more reliable network, and the maintenance headaches of individual power systems are avoided. Similarly, specially designed and safeguarded "computer farms" holding thousands of systems and their data have been built to facilitate what we now call cloud computing.

Knowledge Workers

When the term *knowledge worker* was coined over fifty years ago, people could not have imagined how expanded access to knowledge and information would change our habits. Today's knowledge worker cannot do tasks with just the knowledge in biological memory and what is available in books and other documents. The ability to navigate the internet and to access, select, and index specific information determine one's ability to do true knowledge work. Just a few years ago, modern knowledge workers were thought of as a specific, limited population that included teachers, researchers, librarians, information systems professionals, lawyers, physicians, engineers, and scientists. With the rise of WIC, an increasingly large percentage of society is becoming a set of knowledge workers and knowledge users. Knowledge workers need to access and process information in any kind of work. It is likely that people who do not belong to any of these knowledge-based groups by 2020 will represent a new caste of the underprivileged. They will do work that does not have knowledge worker requirements.

The six features of WIC enable us to communicate in unprecedented ways and to access information previously available to only a privileged few. WIC facilitates the spreading and sharing of ideas and knowledge by giving people both voice and access, including those who were previously shut out due to language barriers and lack of means. This is a new, internet-based Republic of Letters. The original Republic of Letters included hundreds of well-educated intellectuals who contributed to the emergence of the Renaissance. The new Republic of Letters created by WIC has already influenced people in the Middle East to demand freedom and equality. In the past, radio and television influenced large numbers of people, but today, WIC offers more timely and directed communication. It has the distinguishing feature of altering the public's participation habits. In a sense, it is the first step toward the new information democracy. WIC-enabled communication cannot easily be controlled by authorities, so people can express opinions about articles, politics—just about everything. Shocking comments from extremes and reasonable comments from moderates are both allowed. Will the democratic process sort this out and lead us to a more rational society? Time will tell. Whatever the outcome, it is a time of lively and invigorating information exchange.

Criticism

There is criticism each time a new information technology is introduced. Writing and documentation would supposedly ruin the skill of memorization. Gutenberg's moveable type created systems where publishers made printing decisions based on marketing and profit motives. People were, and still are, concerned that information would be distorted to achieve commercial goals. Television, first heralded as a stimulus for improving knowledge and intelligence, is increasingly criticized for its mostly low-quality entertainment, its meager intellectual content, its encouragement of passivity, and its effects on health. The calculator was criticized as a gateway to the "unlearning" of basic mathematical brain processing.

Today, criticism is directed toward the internet, but it is only one component of the new world information community. Some fear that users will get hooked on the internet, sitting for hours in front of the computer, but the same criticism is directed at users of any virtual entertainment, particularly those who watch TV in excess.

Computer programs offer users a wide range of possibilities. These include internet surfing and learning through online searches or reading blogs, but also games. A 2010 survey shows that networking and gaming dominate internet activities.[7] Access to much on the internet is determined by interests, habits, and belief systems. A game that is fun for some is a value-spoiling, youth-seducing motivator of violence for others. Efforts to create more games that stimulate people to acquire valuable information and skills are ongoing. For example, games that encourage users to do fitness exercises, improve their nutrition, or collaborate to solve a larger problem have shown some success.

Some have criticized the internet's potential effect on information processing and resulting behavior. Some people seek information that simply confirms their beliefs, and some complain if they do not find their belief system positioned as they prefer. More open-minded people seek facts and counter facts. Kevin Kelly described his experience on the internet: "For every accepted piece of knowledge I find, there is, within easy reach, someone who challenges the fact. Every fact has its antifact."[8] We have to remind ourselves that the internet allows people to gather information that they believe is correct and most consistent with their belief system. Can education

---

7   Nielsen Wire. http://blog.nielsen.com/nielsenwire/online_mobile/what-americans-do-online-social-media-and-games-dominate-activity/.

8   Kevin Kelly, *The Waking Dream: Is The Internet Changing the Way You Think? The Net's Impact Our Minds and Future,* ed. John Brockman (New York: Harper Perennial, 2011), 18.

teach how to compare beliefs about each issue? Doing so would help people to be better informed and more balanced.

Through the internet, people have the option of comparing information from multiple sources, instead of getting it only through a regional or political newspaper of a specific political bent. It would be nice to have a kind of compass that describes the location of any information source within the landscape of beliefs, information, and opinion. Whether people take advantage of the internet opportunity to compare views, or choose to stay within their comfort zone, remains to be seen.

Another criticism of the internet is that it encourages quick information sessions. Writer Nicolas Carr claims that the internet seems to be "chipping away [his] capacity for concentration and contemplation".[9] People complain that they have gotten out of the habit of reading long books because of the internet. Conversely, others report reading *more* books as a result of the digital publishing movement. People also complain that the internet is causing people to acquire superficial perceptions, to avoid "deeper thinking," to minimize research, and to stay busy rather than reflect deeply.

I have observed a relationship between the intensity of information processing and other activities. The level of thinking appears to decrease with hard labor, distraction, and activities such as singing or fighting. Deep thinking is less likely while one watches entertaining TV, but one might be stimulated by a program about current events or an interview addressing a timely or personal issue. In the same way, some internet programs stimulate thought, while others, like some games and other quick-action interactive programs, obstruct it. The internet has so many options that its effect depends on how people use it.

The perceived economic value of the information industries is a point for debate. Economist Tyler Cowen laments the internet's lack of universal acceptance, because there is a segment of the population that does not participate fully in the information society; it is skeptical of computers, the internet, and mobile devices beyond

---

9   Nicholas Carr, *The Shallows: What the Internet is Doing to Our Brains* (New York: W. W. Norton & Company, 2010), 6.

the basic cell phone.[10] He also states that many of the inventions of the last centuries (electricity, refrigerator, washing machine, dishwasher, etc.) brought clear benefits to buyers, but internet benefits are not so obvious. In fact, however, growth factors for all industries widely depend on the use, integration, and implementation of information technologies. There is no major automobile producer that does not incorporate the latest computer gadgets. No kitchen appliance manufacturer will survive without integrating the latest chips. No business can reject information technologies and survive.

The point of this argument is that most of the devices introduced in the twentieth century were mechanical perfections of earlier inventions. It is easy to forget that any new invention takes time to capture the market. It took thirty years for 80 percent of the population to adopt electricity. The same is true of the electric stove, the air conditioner, and the clothes dryer. The telephone took sixty years, as did the automobile. By comparison, information devices such as radio, color TV, VCR, personal computer, and the internet reached the 80 percent mark within ten years.[11] The mobile phone has been implemented faster worldwide than any technology device in history.

The sophisticated computerization of WIC systems is changing the world, but is this change for the better or for the worse? Some people get very excited about each new technology, expecting a better world to result automatically. But this is not a given. Technology does not bring better life conditions by itself; it could even have a negative impact. The same can be said about information: more does not make us wiser, nor does it prevent us from destructive action. Belief systems and values are influenced by knowledge and information, but information systems are individual, leading in turn to decisions and actions. In other words, WIC is an exciting development, but it is only a tool.

---

10   Tyler Cowen, *The Great Stagnation: How America Ate All the Low-Hanging Fruit of Modern History, Got Sick, and Will (Eventually) Feel Better* (New York: Dutton, 2010).

11   C Peter Waegemann and Claudia Tessier, *The Impact of mHealth* (Boston, MA: mHealth Initiative, 2010).

Behavioral Changes

One of the biggest criticisms of internet and mobile data communication is that a person is online far too much of the time, receiving and responding to messages. Email and text messages come from colleagues, bosses, professional peers, family members, or acquaintances at all hours. Senders often expect fairly quick responses. Many people object to this intrusion into their private lives. They want leisure time when they don't have to respond to an email, text message, or phone call. Also, many complain that they do not have adequate time to think over an electronic communication as they did with paper mail. This is one of the major changes effected by digital communication. It requires a different style of information processing, including communicating in shorter, more precise messages.

At issue here is the value placed on communication as well as our attitude toward the inner self. Silent time can be beneficial for our personal information processing systems, but in an active society, noncommunication is a luxury in which only a few indulge. Very few would want to miss an important message, such as news of an accident or death, even when it comes in the middle of the night. Today's information society brings the constant demand for rapid information exchange. Communication management is part of knowledge capital management and includes finding time for oneself.

Smartphones enable a user to distinguish callers with different ring tones. People can create ecommunities, identifying those who can call anytime, while communication from others will not be accessed until it is convenient. Such communication management may even cross technologies. For instance, I spend a great deal of time at conferences where I cannot easily accept phone calls or listen to voice messages. Therefore, I subscribe to a program that automatically transcribes voice messages and delivers them by email, which I can read without disturbing the meeting or leaving the room.

The changes in written communication styles are already profound. Soon after the introduction of email, millions of people transitioned to messages without traditional letter attributes: many emails have no salutation, complimentary closure, or signature—and most have no guarantee of data integrity. As with any new medium and any new technology, there is mistrust. Common wisdom has it that email is not safe, because people can redirect messages, fake sender addresses, even alter the content. Nevertheless, its utilization is widespread.

After more than a decade, email is going through a major transition. Buying thousands or millions of email addresses is cheap, and sending to such a large number is free or very inexpensive. Therefore, email has become a vehicle for advertising products or services, many of a personal nature. The result is the junk mail syndrome: almost every email subscriber receives unwanted, misleading, annoying, and sometimes upsetting junk messages. More seriously, messages may carry viruses, have criminal intent, or cause financial loss. For these reasons, many people are switching to other communication systems, such as texting and social media communication, as well as secure email systems. Communication filter settings need to protect against the loss of important messages in junk filters, allowing through only important or desired communications. Appropriate digital communication management is a part of knowledge capital management.

Few people would have predicted at the end of the twentieth century that research would become a major, everyday activity for most people. Because of the wealth of information on the internet (and available through mobile phones), many people, including children and students, have become accustomed to basic research on routine matters. "What should we do tonight?" "Let me see what options we have for movies." "Let me find out what special flavors the stores have today." "Let me check the bus or train schedule." "Let me check availability at the golf course."

Control

Powerful rulers, governments, and religious and other organizations have tried to control the flow of, access to, and content of information for thousands of years. Whoever recorded information according to their belief system would "create history": their version of events would be delivered to future generations as fact. Other versions, true or not, were suppressed. Those in power decided what would be promoted as truth, and contradicting information was erased (destroyed, burned, or even chiseled off stone). Books were burned. Even today, some consider certain topics taboo, while other information is considered "politically incorrect." Internet access to some of these may be restricted, while "counter information" is distributed on websites, videos, and in other media.

The biggest complaint about the internet, and rightly so, concerns values. For instance, the most basic human motivator, the sex drive, motivates people of all ages to seek stimuli. A wide range of explicit sexual images and writing is available on the web from countries around the globe, so it is hard to control. As with books and movies, the new digital medium provides access to information that some might consider interesting, while others consider it sinful or disgusting, poisonous smut. In the past, it was easier for authorities to regulate access to this kind of information. For instance, secret museums hide erotic art and literature from the public by order of governing authorities. The internet is not as easily controlled by institutions or authorities, although several countries, including North Korea and China, have implemented substantial restrictions. In general, information is not as easy to control as it was before WIC. Therefore, it is up to the end user, or those protecting users (such as families, schools, churches, or libraries) to restrict such information. This is a major change, as societies are used to having authorities control information that does not fit into their value or belief system. In the new open society, it is up to individuals and communities to make undesired information unavailable. Commercial software is available for this purpose.

While there may be a substantial consensus regarding the management of pornographic information, it becomes more complicated when authorities want to control other types of information. Six hundred years ago, the Catholic Church didn't want lay people to read the bible. Sixty years ago, patients were not allowed access to medical books in many publicly funded libraries, because it was thought that such information could cause harm.[12] Some physicians still resist giving patients access to all of their medical record information. Keeping information secret gives people power. It can be based on beliefs that others cannot understand the information, that they may behave inappropriately in response to it, or that they may be harmed by it. The internet is breaking down this barrier, for better or worse. To manage information, one must be prepared to provide an increasing number of people access to it, even when such access was previously denied. This freedom of information will increasingly be controlled at the user level according to belief systems. A religious fundamentalist, for example, could install semantic commercial filters that block any information that does not fit with particular beliefs.

The general trend is toward greater transparency. WIC has already had some impact on the freedom of information, since it is difficult for rulers and governments to control. The meaning of "publishing" expanded when people began to discuss issues publicly on blogs. Whereas editors controlled what was published in the past, bloggers can freely state opinions and attract a sympathetic (or at least interested) audience. Now everyone can be heard in blogs, comments, and reviews. For instance, anyone can post about an experience with a restaurant or other service provider. This type of public judgment is expanding to other areas as people use smartphone cameras to capture events on the street or something they disapprove of in their organization. This is the ultimate democratic communication option, allowing everyone's voice to be heard. Of course, it can be abused if worthless, misleading, harmful, or untruthful information is posted. Thus, systems that can filter such messages are developing. Any unhappy or former employee or company associate has the power to easily disclose information about certain events or conditions. As will be addressed later, WikiLeaks is just the very beginning of a movement that releases internal organizational communications to the public.

---

12   C Peter Waegemann, *Patient Records: Access and Privacy Issues* (Boston, MA: Medical Records Institute, 2005).

Three types of information control, however, persist: attempts to stop the free flow of *protected information*, of *proprietary information*, and of *poisonous information*.

Protected information is information that could harm a government, an organization, or a person. For instance, it could be something a nation's enemy could use against it or that might cause a person to do harm. While there may be a valid reason to keep such information secret, it leads to the most abuse because it is easy to use "security" as an excuse to withhold information when in fact only the interests of authority are protected. In significant national cases, the public is better served by immediate transparency and release of all information rather than a pretense of protection. For instance, the initial secrecy around the September 11 tragedy led to unanswered questions and conspiracy theories. Open information policies would have benefited both the government's image and the public's concern.

With increasing opportunity for information leaks, governments and others have to change their policies. Managing information capital with policies of openness and transparency is better than old secrecy practices. It improves an organization's image and is more responsive to citizens, clients, and others. Information freedom and information transparency can be compared to the desire for political and personal freedom that will always motivate people. In the corporate world, open information processes can create brand loyalty and customer satisfaction. A student may want to know the reason for a grade and how it compares to others'; a bank client may want to find out why an application was declined; the citizen would like to find out why the town administration has ruled against a request; and so on.

Proprietary information is a major asset, particularly in corporations. It must be maintained, expanded, and protected. It results from investments in resources that benefit an organization. One way to think of proprietary information is "any information that can be charged for." The news media industry, for example, is increasingly being faced with the question: What is special? That is, what can be charged for? If information is reported from the perspective of a specific belief system, then information users looking for that perspective may be prepared to pay for it. However, generic reporting of news may not warrant a charge.

Poisonous information motivates people to acts of terrorism or other violence. If such information cannot be managed sufficiently through counterargument, then controlling or prohibiting it is necessary.

Outside of these three information categories, most information control may be difficult to justify; control may do more harm than good.

It should also be noted that information can be hijacked and changed. Email may appear to be coming from someone else, a website may be set up to imitate the original, or information's source may be obscured. WIC allows many distortions of authenticity. This is the negative effect of openness and lack of control. Anyone can post opinions, write a blog, or pretend to be someone else.

Advanced Intelligence with WIC

Future advanced intelligence will be defined by three factors. The first is the change from relying on our own memory (and, to a limited extent, on books and other materials) to outsourcing much of the memory function to WIC. In this context, digital intelligence will mean the ability to smartly navigate the immense world of knowledge and information, not trying to memorize it. The second factor is the judgment of the value of information. Information that fits into the user's belief systems will be identified as worthy of retention. Information from outside the user's belief systems that is of interest, or is needed, may also be considered valuable. Third, advanced intelligence means using more tools to achieve a higher level of creativity and information management.

It will take time to understand the first factor. In the past, knowledge was brain-centric. Now, the inflection point has been reached, where knowledge is increasingly network-centric. The human mind is the driving force behind it, but it has a significantly smaller memory than the volume of knowledge and information processing it controls.

Knowledge becoming network-centric emphasizes the second factor. Determining the value of information from the huge volume available is going to be a key component of information management. Our belief systems must integrate concepts with data checking mechanisms.

The brain will be the context driver that, with will and energy, manages knowledge. Information, combined with functionality, will increasingly guide people through the use of tools to achieve greater creativity and improved information management. This third factor is already being demonstrated with computer-driven devices that accompany and support us through daily and professional activities. Smartphone applications that remind about appointments, send a prompt to take medication, help to find a restaurant, stimulate to go to a concert, and provide updated news to the minute, are just a few of their services.

As another example, geographic intelligence is one of the oldest intelligence systems for guiding humans on this planet. It is only one of many software "departments" in the brain. It governs our skills in memorizing scenes and patterns in the landscape, which were originally in reference to the sun and the stars. Until the Middle Ages, land and sea travelers used basic navigational tools, memory, and/or narrative descriptions or teachings to avoid getting lost. Later, people absorbed the skill of geographic representation by creating and reading geographic information on maps. Geographic representation developed its own rules, symbols, and a very different information representation system than that of language. Early maps were often misleading and incomplete, but later they improved with validation by other travelers and by comparison to other maps. By the end of the twentieth century, the entire planet had been mapped and topographical information added. Anyone could purchase the resulting maps for accurate navigation by foot, car, bus, train, ship, or even airplane, although they could be expensive. At the beginning of the digital era, images from satellites began to provide map validation. Corrections and improvements continue. Digital maps may even reflect customized usability data. The "shortest distance between two points" may be replaced by "the easiest" or "with the least traffic" or "most scenic" or "safest," or some other criterion-based route according to user preferences.

Stand-alone global positioning systems (GPS) and smartphone navigation, computing, and communication devices are only the first examples of the third factor in this planet's overall knowledge development: the focus on concepts, meanings, and relationships. A person's memory becomes secondary as the user acquires information not from the brain or printed maps, but from a computer system. However, when several routes are offered, the brain determines which to take. It selects the geographical target and decides how to use the information the system offers.

Such a small system may be housed on a digital companion that most people can carry with them. The geographical information housed in the smartphone used in the car or on a bicycle helps one to navigate. The artificial voice of the computer guides the user, specifying where to go and when to turn: how to get to a specific destination. And all of this can be done without the traveler using memory as the primary resource. The memory has become complementary to the GPS. In early navigation systems, people complained that the computer system did not know shortcuts or smaller roads. Some of those complaints persist. One of the new apps lets the user be an active provider of information, reporting (by voice and in real time) traffic conditions, accidents, police traps, and even map corrections. Therefore, new GPS systems are not just replacing geographic memory. They also address changes in traffic flow and road conditions. It is likely that the geographic section of our intelligence (our memories of places, streets, and other geographical data points) will adapt as a result of our dependence on GPS. We may lose the impulse to memorize streets and other data points beyond those we regularly use, since our brains recognize that the digital companion will remember for us. The brain contains many intelligence systems that work side by side. Some may expand while others shrink, over a lifetime. Our geographic intelligence system may be among those that shrink.

Memory and communication applications, based on computer-stored memory with internet communication, will not just create validated knowledge. They will also guide people in many professional and personal functions. Information fields such as medicine, law, engineering, and even language translation may ultimately be mapped like geography, using software to guide people accordingly. A direct line in human development runs from intelligence based solely on the brain to the information society in which the brain, in a sense, is a biological node with limited computing capabilities but with a potential to excel in creativity and motivation.

The new frontier of WIC is neither automatically a wonderful thing, as some claim, nor a negative development as others believe. Rather, it creates both new challenges and new opportunities, and it must be managed, as shown in the following chapters.

2

Information Processing and Communication: The Path to WIC

Human information processing and communication have evolved over tens of thousands of years, increasingly distinguishing humans from other living beings. First, the expansion of thinking led to the ability to transform memorized information into knowledge. Pattern recognition and contextual understanding became key skills to support intelligence. Second, the use of artificial memory—writing and creating documents and books—provided an important and major adjunct to brain memory. The third development, the transition from brain-centric information storage to internet-based (systems-centric) knowledge management, has just begun.

As people enter the new WIC era, which is a global community approach to information management, several questions must be addressed. If information is the ingredient that defines who we are, then how did we get to this level of complex information processing capability? Let me argue that several stages can be identified along the way to our becoming an information society. They may not have occurred discretely or in the sequence described, but they represent the path to theoretical thinking and consciousness, a path that includes both advances in communication and information processing.

Stage 1: How Information Made Us Human: Thinking Processes

Definitions of life abound. For the purpose of this book, consider that life exists when an organism can actively use and manage information to find food, survive, and reproduce. This principle applies to all living organisms, from microorganisms to humans. Animals and other living beings are pretty good at using information to find food, to reproduce, and to learn new ways to survive as their living conditions change. Those organisms that do not have the necessary information to survive and do not manage it to their advantage become extinct.

The capability of managing information translates into survival, and it can also lead to success and even dominance. We humans are disadvantaged when compared to birds, which can fly, or some ocean creatures that can swim long distances. At the same time, we have advantages over these beings. By managing scientific and technical information, we can fly much higher and faster than birds, and we can navigate the oceans above and below the surface. These examples demonstrate how beings can overcome biological and environmental limitations and challenges by acquiring valuable information that is transformed into intelligence.

Our ancestors managed information better than other beings. They memorized where to find shelter and food while hunting and gathering—initially, perhaps, as a squirrel does today. People have debated for centuries why humans developed more of an intellect than other animals, but there is no consensus. Donald R. Griffin describes remarkable examples of animal thinking and toolmaking.[13]

---

13 Donald Griffin, *Animal Minds* (Chicago: University of Chicago Press, 1992).

Several factors contribute to this human transformation. The first is still being researched and debated: What made people go beyond the need to find food and protect themselves? Steven Pinker describes four criteria for this step.[14] He places significant emphasis on sight. What we see is, of course, a major part of the information we acquire. Some 38 percent of all nerve fibers that enter and leave the brain connect to our eyes.[15] This argument must acknowledge that, while the eyesight of birds is generally much better than that of humans, it has not been established that birds have made the first step to manage information beyond their need for food, survival, and reproduction. Animals may have ways to anticipate upcoming environmental events such as storms or flooding, but one cannot imagine their keeping and analyzing records of such events or questioning whether a bird-god was their cause.

Pinker notes that group living could be a second prerequisite. It requires increased communication, generally considered to be one of the criteria for higher intelligence. However, many animals also live in large groups with strict rules, yet they do not break through the glass ceiling of theoretical thinking and consciousness. Bees and ants manage their social interactions through a superorganism, where a specific function is assigned to each member from slaves to queens and from fighters to food growers. Birds communicate with some sophistication and develop certain rules. Many other animals live in large groups and sometimes seem to have a higher collective intelligence than those living alone, but that intelligence does not reach the tipping point that leads to theoretical thinking.

Another factor for human development, according to Pinker and others, may have been the use of the hand—particularly the thumb. The skillful use of our hands offered the possibility of creating tools and, of course, enabled writing. While the use of the hand helped in crafting and using tools, it cannot be the key factor for becoming an exceptionally intelligent being. A number of animals, including chimpanzees, use their" hands" to manipulate primitive

---

14   Steven Pinker, *How the Mind Works* (New York: W. W. Norton & Company, 1997), 191.

15   Juan Enriquez and Steve Gullans, *Homo Evolutis* (TED Books: Kindle Single Edition, 2011) location 1500.

tools, but they have not advanced to other "human" functions such as writing.

Pinker and others also believe that hunting enabled more thinking. Many animals spot, hunt, and devour their prey with remarkable skill, but we are not aware that these animals "think" beyond the need to eat and to address other biological needs. But prehumans did: There are signs that the Australopithecines, *Homo erectus*, archaic sapiens, Neanderthal, and other primates were using information in a more sophisticated way than other beings of their eras. It is likely that early human settlements, which involved first attempts at agriculture, helped move us toward a more advanced life. Settlements encouraged communication, advance planning, memory and storage abilities, rules for togetherness, and opportunities for deeper thinking. However, there is no conclusive agreement on what made human ancestors break through the threshold and start thinking beyond their daily needs.

Therefore, the question remains: What stimulated the step toward abstract thinking among hominids? While we continue to look for answers, two factors may help us understand the move beyond the concerns of the animal information processing system.

The first is creativity in response to challenges, as described by Robert J. Sternberg.[16] Could curiosity have led to creative thinking? What might have challenged prehumans to think outside the box of food, shelter, sex, protection, survival, and aggression? Sternberg suggests that intelligence includes not only memory and analytical abilities, but also creative and practical abilities.[17] Creativity occurs when a person or animal thinks differently than others and converts these different thoughts into new solutions. This often occurs in direct relationship to challenges. When we are forced to find alternative solutions, information processing must abandon conventional thinking.

Creative problem solving is not unique to humans. I personally observed a "solution war" between an engineering-inclined person and a squirrel. After placing a bird feeder on a pole, a man observed

---

16 Robert J Sternberg, *Wisdom, Intelligence, and Creativity Synthesized* (Cambridge, UK: Cambridge University Press, 2003).
17 Ibid., 69.

that a couple of squirrels ate all the seeds and did not allow birds to partake. Both man and squirrel tried to innovate solutions to achieve their opposing goals. The man applied intelligence and engineering skills to create a system to keep the squirrel from the feeder. The squirrel kept trying new ways to overcome these barriers and succeeded each time.

For our ancestors, the challenges of daily living led to knowledge acquisition. The skills to manage fire and to cooperate in hunting larger and more powerful animals had to be learned. Later, farmers and tradesmen taught their sons by example. Skills might include how to farm or how to make shoes, work with metals, or mill grain. But these information acquisitions are still responses to the challenge of daily living.

The historian Arnold J. Toynbee asks, "What is the essential difference between the primitive and the higher societies? It does not consist in the presence or absence of institutions, for institutions are the vehicles of the impersonal relations between individuals in which all societies have their existence, because even the smallest of primitive societies is built on a wider basis than the narrow circle of an individual's direct personal ties."[18] He described any progress or development as the result of a challenge.

If early developments most likely were the result of a challenge, what was the challenge? There were probably several. Basic communication, including language, was needed to hunt and live cooperatively. The thumb helped create effective weapons some fifty thousand years ago. Shortages of food forced hominids to migrate into more challenging climates and to attack larger and more powerful animals; this could only be done with weapons and cooperation.

What could be other stimuli for going beyond the thought system of daily food gathering and trapping, small-time hunting, and becoming concerned with theoretical issues? Kirkpatrick Sale considers the emergence of art: "[Art] is a very practical, indeed vital, product of peoples who were in severe crisis, facing a serious threat to their survival, and who developed this extraordinary means of

---

18   Arnold J Toynbee, *A Study of History*. Excerpt available at http://www.cooperativeindividualism.org/toynbee_challenge_and_response.html.

ritual and magic to allow them to get through this exigency."[19] It is very difficult to extract from spears, bones, and other excavated objects what life was like thirty to a hundred thousand years ago, but art from seventy to a hundred thousand years old provides some evidence.[20] Two engraved ochre stones found in South Africa show animal drawings comparable to cave art produced sixty to ninety thousand years later in Europe. While the need to express emotions, feelings, wishful thinking, or fear may have contributed to the development of human information processing, the main push may instead have come from another development specific to humans, namely trying to understand the unknown or supernatural, i.e., the world of God.

The human race has a violent history. When we consider historical events such as the Holocaust, the Spanish settlers' treatment of the cultures of Central and South America, or the treatment of Native American Indians in North America—to mention a few of the atrocities of human history—it doesn't make sense to assume that early hominids were more civilized than later ones. Some historians describe the "unlikelihood of there having been much reason to kill these hominids for food,"[21] but I find it likely that they killed them for using their women, stealing preserved food, or just to dominate them. Or, if they didn't kill them, they took them as slaves. "Slavery was a major institution in antiquity. Prehistoric graves in Lower Egypt suggest that a Libyan people of about 8,000 BC enslaved a Bushman or Negrito tribe."[22] It was customary for societies around the globe to capture those who could not defend themselves due to inadequate weaponry or other circumstances.

People have always killed other beings and each other; in this regard, they are without equal among animals. Thus, the need to manage human aggression was very important: If people wanted to

---

19   Kirkpatrick Sale, *After Eden: The Evolution of Human Domination*. (Durham: Duke University Press, 2006), 93.

20   Stanley I. Greenspan and Stuart G Shanker, *The First Idea: How Symbols, Language, and Intelligence Evolved from Our Primate Ancestors* (Cambridge, MA: Da Capo Press, 2004), 172-173.

21   Kirkpatrick Sale, *After Eden: The Evolution of Human Domination*. (Durham: Duke University Press, 2006), 618.

22   Hugh Thomas, *The Slave Trade*. (New York: Simon& Schuster, 1997), 25.

live together, they needed to discipline those who expressed their aggression through violence. Social living also presented another, related problem. How can the tribe be motivated toward tasks such as war or hunting larger animals? As societies grew, what could help rulers and leaders to govern and motivate people? When hardship confronted a tribe, what would give people hope and trust that it would get better, stimulating their energy and helping them to survive?

Belief in a supernatural force served these needs in varying ways. The supernatural may have provided a breakthrough, answering a need to understand death and the larger meaning of life's events. Religious images, statues, and belief systems also helped to scare off enemies. Early priests and other religious leaders helped to manage those who displayed the full range of human rage and urges, which required more effective means than brute strength and fighting skills. The belief system around a supernatural force was stronger than a club for discipline. Such a system required interpreting information and developing theoretical thinking that was more complex than what most people could comprehend. Thus, they could "believe," "trust," and "hope" in the supernatural system.

There is evidence that mystic thought was known among groups of prehumans. It has been argued that "wild water buffalo, cattle, camels, and even goats and sheep were initially captured for the sacrifice rather than food."[23] If animals were used to serve the supernatural before being used as food, early concern with the supernatural may have been strong. A cloud, a tree, an unusually formed rock, a body of water, a special animal, a mountain, a unique sky formation, or other significant image could become an imaginary force. Belief in one or more supernatural forces can be seen as a major step toward thinking beyond the daily needs of animal intelligence.

Thinking about the supernatural might also have stimulated early attempts toward an understanding of self and the world. In other words, it may have come from curiosity and led to consciousness. The search to explain setbacks, unusual occurrences, even death, may have led to the conclusion that there is a supernatural

---

23   Kenneth F Kiple and Kriemhield Coneè Ornelas, *The Cambridge World History of Food.* (Cambridge, UK: Cambridge University Press, 2000), 3.

power. This also may have led to a clearer recognition of who one is, leading in turn to consciousness. Their sequence may have been variable, but these steps could have been part of the transition to beings that process information differently than most animals. Of course, this development took a long time, starting perhaps a hundred thousand years ago with some basic recognition of and "interaction" with supernatural forces. By seven to ten thousand years ago, full religious belief systems with multiple gods supported the leading cultures and governments.

Steven Mithen defined religious belief systems with four components: "(1) the belief in a non-physical being; (2) the belief that a non-physical component of a person may survive after death; (3) the belief that certain people within a society are likely to receive direct inspiration or messages from supernatural agencies, such as gods or spirits; (4) the belief that performing certain rituals in an exact way can bring about change in the natural world."[24] He states that there were transient religious ideas between thirty thousand and a hundred thousand years ago, although early supernatural visions might not have had clear expressions. Since thirty thousand years ago, the human mind has used religious ideas and religious institutions as cultural anchors. This provided the basis of modern religion, science, and culture. "The Judeo-Christian tradition, for example, offers explanations for much of the subject matter now studied by biology and psychology."[25]

Religious institutions, even in their beginnings, were major enablers of theoretical thinking and complex information processing. They were also places where language and writing developed. Temples and monasteries initiated research in mathematics, astronomy, language and writing skills, and early natural sciences. Today, one can only be amazed by the grandeur of religious sites like Stonehenge in the United Kingdom, the Moai on Easter Island, or the Temple of Karnak in Egypt. These are examples of early religious expressions that covered the planet in many forms and at different

---

24   Steven Mithen, "Symbolism and the Supernatural," in *The Evolution Culture*, ed. Robin Dunbar, Chris Knight and Camilla Power (New Brunswick, NJ: Rutgers University Press, 1999), 149.
25   Steven Pinker, *The Blank Slate* (New York: Viking, 2002), 1.

times. They were essential to the development of intelligence, culture, and knowledge. Without religious breeding places for abstract thinking, researching, and recording, the advanced state of our society could not have been achieved. Many supernatural forces evolved into multiple gods, merging into or being replaced by single-god religions.

Therefore, some might make the case that it was a god that created intelligence and granted it to early humans. Much scientific knowledge was developed in the mainly religious research centers of the time, such as the temples of Sumer or Egypt, Christian monasteries such as Montecassino in Italy, and later in religious places throughout Europe and in other regions of the world. In these "learned" places, a triad of information storage was created: memorizing, complementing memory with reading, and making personal notes. These three processes were the mark of a true scholar.

Memory as Basis of Intelligence

It is likely that concern with the supernatural intertwined with another key human development as emerging emotions formed motivations and drivers for daily life. Consider anger and revenge as motivators. They provide the impulsive energy to fight. Some animals, too, seem to have such motivators. Elephants appear to have internal motivators for revenge as well as for sorrow. Of course, more research is needed to find out whether owls and lions have a sense of pride, chickens have empathy for others, or cows have hope. Such suggestions appear ridiculous at first glance, but we do know that many animals have a sense of fear. The refinement of emotions in early human development may have contributed to the development of intelligence, the expansion of memory, and higher information processing capabilities. In addition, emotions influence internal energy—giving force through joy, for example, or depleting energy through depression or sadness.

As a part of this developmental process, early prehumans had to be able to store information by simple brainpower, that is, without artificial or external help; they had to recognize valuable information and memorize it for later use and/or transmission to others. Memory was used to teach others, to settle disputes, to repeat what was successful in hunting, and to find one's way back home. It brought humans to an advanced stage of functioning. To this day, intelligence is measured by the ability to code important information, memorize it, put it into context, combine it with other memorized or newly encountered information, and use or transmit it when the appropriate occasion occurs. Like a computer's memory, human memory enables the processing of information. Complex information processing and the storage and retrieval of information must work well together for maximum effect. What makes humans unique in the animal kingdom is the sum of information skills in the neurological field of our brain.

Increased intelligence involves absorbing information, identifying and memorizing data deemed important, and establishing context. The result is new knowledge that is learned and stored. Altogether, this is a huge task. Absorbing information involves all five senses: seeing, hearing, smelling, feeling, and tasting. It also involves intuitive messages that the mind absorbs. Think of the vibes you get at a meeting or when meeting a stranger. Or consider the exchange of pheromones: chemical odors that help create sexual attraction. Together, your obvious and hidden biological information capture devices bring an unimaginable wealth of information to you, second by second, minute by minute, hour by hour, and day by day throughout your lifetime. People must process basic data that they sense and use pattern recognition capabilities to convert those data into useful information. For example, when you read this text, your brain recognizes characters as data and then puts their patterns together to form words and convert them into meaningful information. The same applies when you look at a picture or a scene in your living room. Pattern recognition connects the many data points our eyes see in order to create a contextually based, meaningful picture for the memory. It also assigns meaning to sounds. Thus, we use each of our senses to collect information, connect the dots, and create knowledge.

Most of this information is used for daily activities and then discarded. However, some is put into permanent memory. The information we are exposed to is so rich that it is impossible to keep more than a tiny fraction of it in our brain. Would it really be meaningful to keep the information of what you saw, heard, smelled, or felt last Wednesday morning between 10:00 and 10:05? Most of the information we sense is not of sufficient significance to store, but some is often remembered as an impression. Over thousands and thousands of years, our mind has developed a system to keep some information for the short term, other information somewhat longer, and still other information much longer, perhaps for life. Our minds are constantly, but mostly unconsciously, deciding the value of information to be stored. What is more important to us is coded for longer-term memory, while what is not valuable can be discarded. We could not function without this separation of observed data; otherwise our minds would be overloaded with everything from trivia to absolutely essential data, with little ability to differentiate.

This process of assigning value to information is also a key to understanding why one student does better during the learning process than another. A number of factors may prevent or inhibit the learning process. Positive reinforcement, for example, can lead a student to be "interested" in a subject. This makes acquisition of information easier. Negative emotional motivators may make it difficult to pay attention or code information for memory, because other brain processes are stronger. The focused learning process of a person reading a text and trying to memorize it also depends on the relevance of the information to be learned. A student may not value learning details of the history lesson, but values the history of a sports team, memorizing who won in what year with what score.

To a great extent, the retained knowledge of a lifetime represents who you are. You distinguish yourself from other people by your knowledge, opinions, values, beliefs, retained experiences, and prejudices, as well as how you convert all of these, along with feelings and emotions, into behavior. Those with more highly developed learning and knowledge acquisition skills and consequent privileges have tended to use them to dominate others. For thousands of years, a two-class system existed in any given time, place, or society—the educated and the uneducated. Opportunities for knowledge acquisition were unequal. They depended on a person's family background, education, station in life, location, and other, mostly uncontrollable, factors. The curious and motivated child of a poor farm worker's family in a remote area had little chance to learn in the same way that a child from a privileged family in the city could.

Prejudices against those who have not had optimal conditions for knowledge acquisition have been abundant. Those who considered themselves smart were quick to label others as ignorant or stupid. They maintained that people with easier learning capabilities had inherited them, had been given such skills by God, or were smarter because they belonged to a special ethnic or social group. In many countries, victims of prejudice were (and often still are) women and people of minority backgrounds. In Europe and North America, people of non-European background were, and to some extent still are, often discriminated against in the judgment of learning capability. Thankfully, these prejudices are in decline. Two hundred, even fifty years ago, it would have been unthinkable for a non-white person to not only become President of the United States of America, but also to be recognized for his knowledge and critical thinking abilities.

Knowledge is intricately linked to communication: Information acquisition (inward) and information transmission (outward) are both based on communication, most obviously reading, writing, and speech. But let us not forget the information that music or a painting transmits or the smells and sounds that we encounter, or even emotional outbursts, which are also forms of communication.

Animals communicate too. "Our primate cousins possess visual and auditory systems similar to ours, form organized societies, and exploit complex systems of communication," states Bénédicte de Boysson-Bardies.[26] "Thus, velvet monkeys warn their community of danger by cries that indicate whether the aggressor is an eagle, a snake, or a cheetah." Communication begins with symbols and simple sounds and, over time, develops into a complex system. Philip G. Chase defines a symbol as "one kind of sign—that is, something

---

26   Bénédicte de Boysson-Bardies, *How Language Comes to Children*, trans. M B DeBevoise (Cambridge, MA: The MIT Press, 1996), 4.

(a gesture, sound, object, image, etc.) that refers to something else. Some signs point to their referents by association, as smoke indicates fire."[27] He states that symbolism is at the heart of language. Symbols are the most basic form of communication. Linguists debate whether Noam Chomsky's Big Bang Theory of language or some theory of step-by-step development will prove correct. About seven thousand natural languages have developed on this planet, with little mapping or interfaces among them.

The divergent evolution of languages was a major problem for universal knowledge development. For thousands of years, scholars yearned for a "lead language." Roman Latin was very influential over the last two thousand years. Much of law, Christian philosophy, medicine, and scientific writing was done in Latin until the early or mid-twentieth century. As a result of the British Empire and the rise of the United States, English now has acquired the role of a world language, the *lingua franca* of the modern era; it has become the language of new computer technologies. Parallel to this development, translation software has reached a point where languages are beginning to be mapped together. Within the next ten or twenty years, both of these developments will strengthen; the importance and use of English will increase, and translation services will become more intuitive and more accurate. This will further expand knowledge; each language has a wealth of information that hitherto has not been available to people who could not read or speak it.

Stage 2: Writing and Books

As language slowly evolved, so did writing. Early graphic communication was through art that depicted animals and other symbols. With the aid of writing, artificial memory was extended through such media as sand, wax, wood, stone, bark, leaves, lead, skins, parchment, papyrus, and paper. This type of expression began approximately seven thousand years ago and required new

---

27   Philip G Chase, "Symbolism as Reference and Symbolism as Culture," in *The Evolution Culture*, ed. Robin Dunbar, Chris Knight and Camilla Power (New Brunswick, NJ: Rutgers University Press, 1999), 35.

skills that impacted societies in many ways. An important segment of the population was growing: those who could write and read. At first, information was dictated to scribes who wrote information into documents, not unlike managers of the twentieth century dictating to secretaries who recorded the information mechanically with typewriters. In early times, writing information by hand for a ruler or superior was time-consuming and resource-intensive. For example, in the twelfth century, ten scribes worked for two years to produce the History of Damascus.[28] In other words, it took twenty years of full-time work to write these books! The largest accumulation of knowledge was the Siku Quanshu, a very ambitious project ordered by the Chinese emperor in the eighteenth century. It reportedly involved over 3,800 scribes and 361 editors.[29] This army of scribes took nine years to create the books, which contained 2.3 million pages.

Why such an effort? The human mind is limited, sometimes subjective, and without much permanence. Memories are subject to emotional influences that modify, reduce, or delete information. Also, emotional motivations and disuse of certain intelligence sectors in the brain lead to general forgetfulness. For the purpose of establishing law and documenting taxes and governance, a more reliable and permanent way of capturing and storing information was necessary. Unlike memorized information, recorded information could not be easily changed. Further, information did not disappear with the death of the person in whose brain it resided; recorded knowledge could be accessed even in the distant future.

Inscribing basic information on stones, wood, and other material was the answer to the shortcomings of human memory. For thousands of years, documents gave contemporaries and subsequent generations knowledge about events. The extent of knowledge accumulation is directly related to the ease of recording. When scribes had to write by hand, knowledge was limited to the very few who had access to their scrolls and documents. The introduction of moveable type printing was a huge improvement for knowledge

---

28   Ann Blair, *Too Much To Know.* (New Haven: Yale University Press, 2010, Kindle edition), 700.

29   Ibid., 775.

distribution. Without it, technology developments and knowledge management could not have advanced at the speed they have. In other words, without the ease of printing books and distributing knowledge through them, we likely would not have automobiles, electricity, telephones, computers, and more.

From priests and specialized scribes to an expanding population of readers and writers, developments moved toward the ideal that every person should learn how to read and write. What appear now as wonderful improvements in human development and information technology were not universally considered a blessing. Writing, publishing, and even note-taking were major steps toward improving information storage and communication, but they also brought change that was not always welcomed. In the same way that some people today rebel against the internet, many people objected first to memorizing and later to writing. The seventeenth century orator Nicolas Malebranche condemned the sciences of memory not only for confusing the mind and disturbing clear ideas but also for inducing pride in the multitude of facts stuffed in one's head.[30]

Similarly, writing was objected to. Plato's arguments from several thousand years ago could well be applied by today's skeptics of the internet. To the statement that "writing and letters will make the Egyptians wiser and give them better memories," Plato's king responds that "this discovery [of writing] will create forgetfulness in the learners' souls, because they will not use their memories; they will trust to the external written characters and not remember of themselves."[31] The king argues that writing and reading are aids not to memory, but to reminiscence, and they give disciples not truth, but only the semblance of it. He claims that people will hear many things but learn nothing; they will appear to know all but will not actually know much of anything; they will be tiresome company, appearing wise but not being so. Doesn't this fit perfectly with some of the arguments made today against the internet?

---

30   Nicholas Malebranche, *The Search after Truth: With Elucidations of the Search after Truth,* ed. Thomas M Lennon and Paul J Olscamp (Cambridge University Press: 1997).

31   Plato, *Phaedrus,* from a translation by B. Jowett, streamlined and altered. http://www9.georgetown.edu/faculty/jod/texts/phaedrus.html.

Writing brought several changes that resonate with our own times. First, writing was (more or less) permanent. Human memory could be increasingly supported by written documentation and by preserving its information beyond one's lifetime. This sounds like the debate about the lack of "forgetfulness" in social media and computer documentation: our inability to permanently erase their information. The fear of being labeled for life by Facebook or other social media entries is widespread. Even the White House discovered that emails that were considered deleted could be recovered. Particularly in Europe, legislation that allows people to erase internet entries after a certain period of time is being considered. It is doubtful that effective laws will result, but commercial processes may be developed to make the internet "forget." In the new information era, it will be important to think twice before recording something. Considering what is going on today with the internet and other new systems, it is understandable that some considered writing "evil."

Second, writing requires a different way of thinking and formulating a message than does speaking. In speech, one can describe thoughts and support them with emotional expressions, and one can repeat, correct, stumble, and mumble in ways that writing does not allow. Writing needs more precision in determining and expressing information intended for a potential reader. In addition, there is the issue of style of communication. It is easier to indulge in a detailed conversation that includes many irrelevant data points than to produce a precise, short written communication. The former is the template many professionals have acquired; the latter is the template that new communication systems require. Professionals, such as lawyers, doctors, and corporate managers, need to switch from a storytelling mode to precise, short, descriptions of their intent in a specific message.

Third, a written information piece is subject to an increased readership (not necessarily intended or authorized), and therefore to increased analysis and criticism. One doctor's anecdote shows how this can work: When he made a misdiagnosis in a lengthy verbal communication with the patient and one or two colleagues, almost no one detected the error. But when an electronic medical record system that required precise entries was introduced, many physicians caught the misdiagnosis and he was corrected. Future organizational transparency requires correct and precise documentation.

Despite resistance, writing and documents became the main enhancement of culture and civilization in much the same way that the internet is transforming our society today. However, past information systems did not allow the ease of access we have today. Some rulers felt that it was important to carry their wealth of knowledge with them. Some sources say that a tenth-century Grand Vizier of Persia, Abdul Kassam Ismael, carried his library with him wherever he went. Four hundred camels carried his 117,000 volumes of books and rolls.[32] A large group of people maintained this mobile library for fairly quick retrieval and managed its indexing and storage. Imagine telling this ruler that, little more than a thousand years later, literally billions of documents would be available to most people through the internet and that the knowledge-retrieval process would require little effort. Could he even comprehend why relatively few people take advantage of this wealth of information?

From Handwritten Books to Printing

In the last five hundred years, most information has been mass-produced; that is, printed. Gutenberg's movable type began a new era of information: it could be printed faster than it could be written. In 1630, it was estimated that four men could print in a day what had taken ten scribes a year to write by quill.[33] Not only could books be produced more efficiently, they also could be distributed to more people. Thus, the knowledge base of populations increased. Books enabled scholars and others to identify information they valued (or were told to value) and place it in long-term memory storage. Although people could memorize information from

---

32   Although no original source is quoted, this entry is listed on a number of websites such as http://interesting.kitt.net/2006/03/abdul-kassam-ismael-grand.html.

33   Ann Blair, *Too Much To Know*. (New Haven: Yale University Press, 2010, Kindle edition), 1180.

books, its volume far exceeded memory capacity. Later, information management skills were developed for categorizing, indexing, and making print information stored in large libraries retrievable. In this way, the intellectual history of humanity—the history of thought in written form—began the journey toward today's body of knowledge. Since books were first printed, context and knowledge that is stored in the mind has interacted with that stored in books.

The Technical Side of Information Storage and Communication Systems

The call for a "paperless society" began around the 1960s. Between 1970 and 2010, tools for easier, correct documentation became commonplace: word processors, spell-checkers, and other digital writing support. Paper printing is slowly declining as digital information becomes more and more prevalent and new storage media benefit individuals and organizations. The adoption and evolution of computer storage devices has been rapid. New devices have become mainstream and old ones obsolete. Information on early floppy disks had to be converted to compact disks (CDs), then CDs were converted to DVDs and USB drives. DVDs became outdated as music, video, and other information moved to storage on computers, iPods, and similar devices. Smartphones and other mobile devices can hold thousands of books and pieces of music that used to be stored on multiple CDs and DVDs. The rise of the network created the move to storage in the cloud. Some larger organizations are moving their storage of organizational knowledge offsite, and consumers are getting used to storing some of their knowledge base in central, but remote, places. Someone may store twenty or thirty books on an ereader, tablet, or smartphone, but the bulk of the book collection may be stored with an ebook management company for at-will access. If bookshelves were once the showpiece of bourgeois living rooms or private libraries the pride of the privileged in the twentieth century, the multimedia network with home screens, portable working tablets, and smartphones are the pride of our times.

The cost of digital storage has plummeted almost incomprehensibly. In 1956, storage of 1 megabyte (MB) cost about $10,000 on an IBM computer. By 1980, 1 MB of storage from another supplier, Morrow Designs, cost $193. Ten years later, the cost of 1 MB was $7; by the year 1999, it had dropped to 1.5 cents. By December 2005, one thousand megabytes—one gigabyte (GB)—cost 59.8 cents, and in 2010, 1 GB cost less than one cent.[34] Digital storage is one of the major drivers of the knowledge revolution. The cost of storage is low, and the convenience of accessing stored information via the network encourages more and more organizations and individuals to become part of this knowledge web.

The Communication Trail

About 5,500 years ago, scribes in Egypt went from village to village to read and write for illiterate inhabitants and to deliver letters to officials and others. This was the very beginning of a postal communication network that peaked in the twentieth century and is on the wane in the twenty-first. The early system connected villages, temples, and the homes of religious and governmental leaders. As postal mail systems matured and spread to other countries over the last centuries, the letter became the main information exchange medium for orders, invoices, payment demands, account statements, government communications, and so on, and for information (about plants, food, alchemical experiments, and discoveries, for example). It also facilitated the communication of belief systems, particularly among members of religious organizations such as missionaries, priests, church, or temple officials. While most of this letter correspondence concerned practical and business matters, increasing literacy empowered private letter "conversations" among friends, family members, lovers, and others who were geographically separated. In the seventeenth and eighteenth centuries, those who were interested in politics, philosophy, theology, new scientific discoveries, and other intellectual issues exchanged their opinions, beliefs, and knowledge through letters. This movement, called the

---

34   For details, see http://www.canadacomputes.com.

"Republic of Letters" in Europe and America, took place among people who often could converse in several languages, and it influenced the Age of Enlightenment. In retrospect, it was a slow and cumbersome predecessor of today's blog culture and social media, where ideas can be exchanged and debated in seconds, independent of location.

It took substantial time for letters and documents to travel between locations. Solutions for quick information transmission included communication via drums in Africa and, in other places, smoke signals, beacons, or reflected light. Telegraphy systems appeared at the very beginning of the nineteenth century in Europe. Like all technological developments, its initial centralized approach gave way to a general one. Cables permitted the transmission of a message within hours, or a day or two. To send a message, a person had to go to a telegraph company's office and provide the staff with a short message to be transmitted. After telegraphy, it was printed out at the receiving location and physically delivered by special messenger. This allowed communication over long distances, across oceans, and between countries. For almost two centuries, the cable was the preferred method for sending an important, time-sensitive message over long distances. In contrast, the telephone system was a distributed approach, allowing any person to communicate by voice with another. The impact of the telephone dramatically changed society, business, and communication in general. Who would have thought that the internet would bring about even more dramatic changes than the introduction of the telephone?

This next step, the development of data and voice transmission over the air, would be a truly amazing wonder to previous generations. With wireless phones, people can be reached outside of fixed locations such as homes and offices. People can call for help in almost any situation and can communicate from remote areas where no wired phone line has been installed. This new phenomenon is only in its infancy, and it will grow and change over the next decade. It empowers users. They can post positive or negative comments about a workplace, a restaurant, a hotel, a car repair shop, the quality of public transportation, or an experience with an airline agent. This is true democracy, where everyone can have a voice and the power to communicate opinions and experiences.

Stage 3: WIC

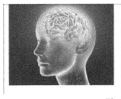

Three Stages of Information Processing

In stage 1, all memory and information processing (thinking) is taking place in the brain.

In stage 2, books and documents supplement the brain. Active interaction occurs between information stored in the brain, information stored in books, and information on notes.

In stage 3, most of the information is stored in WIC. The brain's new role is to
• Navigate the wealth of information
• Create context of much of the data
• Work with artificial intelligence, and
• Select information according to one's belief system.

Figure 2. Three stages of information processing

It is worthwhile to consider how information systems reached their current stage and how a hierarchy of information processing was formed. First, as described above, the transition from animal intelligence systems to theoretical thinking and extensive learning and memorizing can be considered the tipping point in our intellectual development. The second stage brought help for the human brain in the form of writing, books, and documents—an artificial extension of the memory. We are now in the third stage. Memory has grown to such an extent that knowledge on this planet is no longer brain-centric, but systems-centric. There is far more information stored on the internet than any individual can retain or manage. In other words, people are becoming more and more dependent on the information they retrieve (or are fed) from computer-like devices. As noted earlier, one of the first examples of such systems is the global positioning system (GPS) that tells a person how to walk, drive, fly, bike, and so on, to a destination. Similar guidance can be expected in other fields in the near future.

There is also a hierarchy of information use. For most of history, people made daily decisions according to their station in life and the work they did. Some, who lived in temples or were associated with universities and other places removed from the daily challenge of earning a living (working in the fields or doing other labor), could study and interpret bodies of knowledge, such as religion and law. Priests and legal professions were part of this group early on. Others concerned themselves with logic, particularly in mathematics and related fields. Philosophers tried to make sense of this world.

WIC enables storage of information that is massively greater than the brain's capabilities in Stage 1, even greater than the information amassed in libraries. The combination of a new dimension of information storage with increased information processing capabilities through digital tools and artificial intelligence can place human thinking into a new category. A renaissance is possible in which violent, emotional thinking is monitored and moderated, computer-driven machines perform much of the physical labor, and humans become creative knowledge managers.

Epublishing

One of the results of WIC is the new way of knowledge distribution. Ebook publishing and the distribution of knowledge may have an impact on our society similar to that of the introduction of moveable type. Printing offered more people new access to knowledge and opinions. These new printing techniques contributed to the Renaissance, to new thinking about life and democracy, and to expanded scientific activity.

Book publishing was a milestone in information and knowledge development. Critics complained that commercialization might cripple information flow. The spread of an author's work depended on the publisher's evaluation of its marketability. In other words, the estimated market determined whether a book got printed and how it was promoted. Good ideas and interesting new concepts were often overlooked in this commercial system. In addition, the (monetary) value of creating intellectual material was limited, since most of the revenues went toward book production, marketing, distribution, and other costs, with little remaining for either the publisher or the author.

By the turn of the millennium, book publishing had grown into a huge, complex business, controlled by publishers. WIC brought several major disruptive changes in publishing within just a few years. First, the word processing function of computers eased the task of writing books. Rather than writing and correcting on paper, a writer could type or speak to create text, move it around, make insertions, use spell-checking and grammar tools, and use automated functions, such as the creation of indexes and word search and replacement. As a result, more people wrote books. This brought commercial publishers a substantial increase in submissions and publishing requests. As they got overwhelmed with proposals, a new filtering authority was introduced: literary agents. They filtered the flood of manuscripts, matching authors with appropriate publishers. However, they too have been overwhelmed by the sheer number of author queries in the last decade. It can be argued that the current book publishing industry is broken. New authors face severe bottlenecks in the publishing industry. The time is ripe for a dramatic change that may have a huge impact on our civilization: epublishing. It brings new features: (1) Authors who could not get published under the old system can "self-publish." This means participating in or even directing the production and marketing process. (2) Printing on demand means books need not be printed before they are ordered. (3) Digital publishing brings information management advantages to both readers and authors. Readers can look up unfamiliar words, take notes and highlight passages digitally, and take advantage of data linking. Authors benefit from the ease of updating and correcting and from new royalty distribution patterns.

In the world of WIC, information does not have to be printed on paper, and it does not have to be published by traditional publishers. This changes the focus of book production from traditional publishing's costly selection, production, and marketing process, where the author may typically get 10 to 20 percent of the receipts, to digital book production and dissemination. Ebook authors can receive a much higher percentage of book revenues, perhaps as high as 50 to 70 percent. Ebooks are based on electronic editing and production functions, with the attendant benefits of easy updating, remote storage, and information linking. In the world of social media and community-based marketing, ebooks can be promoted to specific groups of interested readers. New marketing methods will include book rentals or chapter rentals, and even the opportunity to buy a book's core information.

Information processing and communication will determine our future just as they have determined our past. Understanding how we got here helps us examine where the current disruptive developments are taking us and how we can most benefit from them. Each stage has enabled us to better understand and manage our planet, and each new stage has had a deeper impact on our lives than the previous one. It is clear that our societies and our lives will never be the same.

3

A New Definition of Intelligence?

W IC changes our understanding of intelligence. Human information processing and storage consists of several intertwined branches. One branch is the development of logic, particularly in mathematics and language.

A second branch of human intellectual development is in maximizing the processes of learning, mainly through memorizing. Human intelligence is based on the accumulation of knowledge. Our natural sciences emerged as people discovered more about the world. Early natural sciences included the study of plants, which grew into the field of botany. The management of fire, the study of its effects, and the study of substances led to the field of chemistry. The study of matter and energy became the field of physics. Information specialists, such as those in monasteries, studied day and night cycles, time, and the constellations. Travelers studied and recorded mountains and landmasses. Others explored oceans, rivers, and lakes. Thus, the bodies of knowledge for astronomy and geography were created, and others such as physics and engineering followed.

A third branch of intellectual development was the interpretation of information and knowledge into religious and philosophical belief systems by early philosophers, priests, and prophets. Some, namely Akhenaton, Moses, Zarathustra, Jesus, Mani, Mohammed, Buddha, Confucius, and Lao-tse, acted as "midwives" for monotheistic messages. These religious and philosophical interpretations represented the values of their day, establishing guidelines for eating, morality, and behavior.

Definitions of Intelligence

As various belief systems developed, Greek and Roman philosophers were challenged to classify information as useful, damaging, or benign in relationship to their belief system. In countries where the Greco-Roman meaning of intelligence persisted, a person who questioned common wisdom and beliefs and who constantly examined knowledge for its validity was often considered an intellectual. Over time, however, the definition of intelligence changed, particularly in the English-speaking world. Early modern philosophers in the English language domain, such as Francis Bacon, Thomas Hobbes, John Locke, and David Hume, considered *understanding* to represent intelligence. *Intelligence* came to mean a combination of two functions: a memory function and an ability to think creatively.

Intelligence also referred to all information processing and storage functions within human development. Since the introduction of writing, the body of recorded knowledge was considered to be at the heart of intelligence. The intellectual history of this planet consists of knowledge incorporated into belief systems. Robert J. Sternberg defines successful intelligence[35] as "the ability to achieve success in life in terms of one's personal standard, within one's sociocultural context." Intelligence "depends on capitalizing on one's strengths and correcting or compensating for one's weaknesses[...] Balancing abilities is achieved in order to adapt to, shape, and select

---

35   Robert J Sternberg, *Wisdom, Intelligence, and Creativity Synthesized.* (Cambridge, UK: Cambridge University Press, 2003), 42.

environments." Successful intelligence is "attained through balance of analytical, creative and practical abilities." With these abilities, one is likely to be successful. But there is more. I would argue that intelligence also has to do with information processing: pattern recognition (particularly in understanding the context of complicated situations), knowledge acquisition skills (such as learning and search navigation expertise), retention and memory capabilities, thinking (including problem solving), and good communication through any media.

One Cattel-Horn-Carroll intelligence theory measures ten abilities, subdivided into seventy narrow abilities.[36] It is an attempt to rate generic capabilities such as fluid intelligence (the capacity to think logically and solve problems in novel situations), crystallized intelligence (accessing skills and memorized information), reading and writing, and memory and processing information. The question of whether we can test *general intelligence* is controversial. Howard Gardner theorized that there are multiple intelligences that are very person- and culture-dependent.[37]

Many studies consider intelligence as an *educated whole*, best described by the German term *Bildung*. Developed particularly during the eighteenth and nineteenth centuries, it was defined as a comprehensive understanding of history, law, theology, and natural sciences. This was only possible in an era when knowledge was limited. No longer can any science researcher absorb a whole field like physics or chemistry; no lawyer can master every section of the law; no doctor can be expert in all the branches of medicine; and so on. The increased sophistication of knowledge has led in most professions to such specialization that we must rethink the notion of a comprehensive intelligence.

Intelligence in a specific field has to change its focus from memorizing knowledge to thinking conceptually and navigating the information system to retrieve appropriate data and information. Appropriate data from WIC may be used to prove or disprove concepts, develop plans, and create new ideas.

---

36   Alan S Kaufman, *IQ Testing 101* (Springer Publishing Company, 2009).

37   Howard Gardner, *Frames of Mind: The Theory of Multiple Intelligences* (New York: Basic Books, 1993).

A person actually has many intelligence systems. Body intelligence manages physical systems and organs. It manages movement and coordinates our biological systems. Professional intelligence includes skills, knowledge, and information processing in our jobs and professions. Driving and traffic intelligence governs safe driving and effective maneuvering in traffic. News intelligence governs the acquisition of political and other news from newspapers, radio, television, websites, and other sources. Current affairs and news influence political and other intelligence systems. Sports intelligence manages all sports information. Health intelligence steers nutritional decisions, exercise choices, environmental influences, hygiene, pain management, and appropriate responses to keep our bodies in shape. Financial intelligence helps us budget and manage money matters. Music intelligence enables a person to read and compose music and play instruments. Social intelligence enables us to get along with others and have positive relationships. Computer and internet intelligence helps us to get the most out of computing and digital networking. Art intelligence opens up the world of visual and auditory arts. And so on. One could easily come up with hundreds of specific intelligence systems a person might excel in or be deficient in, and these main intelligence fields can be further subdivided. For instance, knowing classical tunes and identifying the piece and its composer is a subdivision of music intelligence.

We must also consider what happens when we encounter information overload. The brain has to decide what is important to memorize and what is not. Even further, there are signs that memorized information is placed within a specific hierarchy of importance according to an individual's energy level, interest, emotional motivators, and other factors. Whereas someone may have memory items at a level where details are always recalled immediately, other information may take some time to recall, particularly after accumulating several decades' worth of information.

An intelligence framework could serve as a model for all intelligence systems and as a base for daily functional intelligence. It could also lead to changes in the education process, from emphasizing memorization to emphasizing the management of intelligence in specific subject matter areas. Thus, the challenge for students of any age will be to determine what information fields interest them and match their ability. The selection will determine future professional development. The deeper one delves into these specific knowledge bases, the greater the influence they will have on future professional status, remuneration, and professional success.

An important, yet often overlooked issue is that intelligence requires distinguishing between accurate, incorrect, opinionated, and misleading information. Also important is the constant evaluation of belief systems as they are encountered, identifying which information fits into one's belief system, and, in turn, the selection of information communities. This is true not only with regard to information on the internet, but also to all information, whether in books, other media, from another person, or from other sources. The flexibility and openness to evaluate opinions and prejudices is especially important in the age of WIC.

Consciousness and Intelligence Systems

Human intelligence, therefore, incorporates many fields and subsystems. So far, only intelligence systems that fall into the range of conscious intelligence have been addressed. However, many biological parts and systems have their own intelligence to sense conditions, send messages, and react to events. One way to look at the human body's network of intelligence systems is to consider consciousness itself. Since the late seventeenth century, it has been recognized as a key ingredient of the human mind. It represents, among other things, awareness and a sense of self that animals and other living beings do not appear to have. The concept of consciousness is controversial. Theologians, neuropsychologists, neuropharmacologists, computer scientists, philosophers, computer subject matter experts, and others do not agree on what it is or on what role it has.

Three base stages of consciousness include the vegetative state, the unconscious, and various levels of the conscious state. When people are fully aware and fully conscious, the central processing system is in full control. However, this state is not constant. Full consciousness includes thinking, i.e., the integration of rules for thinking itself, information capture, the recognition of context and/or pattern, and value criteria that filter and produce results. Nonthinking activities are usually reduced to a minimum as the thinking mind consumes attention, energy, and awareness. For routine tasks such as repetitive work or driving on a very straight or familiar road, a modified level of consciousness allows parallel processing of mindful activities with routine. In other words, two or more separate mental activities can be performed. One or more of them may make use of the subconscious, where one can perform an activity without remembering it. Commuters who drive the same route day after day are unlikely to remember any one commute as different from another unless something outside of the routine occurred.

Subconscious information processing also occurs during sleep and "paradoxical sleep," a borderline between wakefulness and sleep. Sleep and brain experts have not reached a consensus on what goes on in the mind when people sleep, and people have tried to interpret dreams for thousands of years.

Each body part and system acquires, processes, and transmits information. The brain has the highest post in the biological federation of body organs, parts, and systems, and traditional understandings of intelligence focus on the brain. The intellect is largely governed by it. I say "largely" because the intellect, when understood as the central information processing and decision system, is also governed by intuitive feelings and emotional motivators that are not part of "rational" thinking processes. Reasoning, on the other hand, includes thinking processes and information storage functions acquired in a conscious and active mode, software-driven will, context and pattern recognition (real and imagined), and the application of logic. They are all part of the brain. But there is more.

For over three thousand years, thought leaders such as Zoroaster, Buddha, Plato, and later philosophers assumed that there is more than the brain: a kind of "brain plus." In their perception, the mind covers information acquisition through senses other than the five familiar ones and retrieval of *learned knowledge from memory*.

Emotions, will, intuition, and unconscious cognitive processes also support the information processing function of thinking.

Of course, awareness of biological communication that parallels and influences the mind did not fully evolve until recently. Just as the microscope enabled scientists to discover the microcosm of the very small, a new worldview of the mind has emerged through scientific research in biochemistry, microbiology, medicine, and other fields. Slowly, we are understanding that much of what influences life is not at the level of human sensors. What we can see, hear, smell, taste, or touch is just the tip of the iceberg and does not give us answers to what drives many actions in this world. Cells have information processing functions, as do microbes, Bacteroidetes, and other organisms. A person, an animal, and a plant consist of many living parts, and each hosts a range of other small beings that participate in the organism's environment. None of them function like an inorganic mechanism—like a watch that does not adapt to changes in the environment or surrounding circumstances. In contrast, mechanical devices driven by computers can respond to changing input.

It might be helpful to think of the community of cells and other small living building blocks of a person, an animal, or a plant as similar to a corporation, government, or other organization. There, many divisions, departments, and individuals have to do cognitive functions to be competitive, to react to changes, and to try to succeed. There is the corporate behavior, the departmental behavior, and the employee behavior, each governed by information capture and storage, information processing, and communication. Much like organizations, there are different places in the brain where, simultaneously, similar biological cognitive functions are going on.

Thus, Frank T. Vertosick Jr.[38] argues that life (in general) is a network of information. His seven levels of life development are based on communication, from the simplest to the complex. Each has information storage and information processing components, but each is limited to the intellectual capacity necessary to solve its problems and to survive—no more and no less. Living cells are networked into organs. An organ in the body is like a department in a large

---

38   Frank T Vertosick Jr, *The Genius Within* (New York, Harcourt, 2002).

corporation. It must ensure the department's efficient functioning using rules and information processing, but its success depends on communication with other departments. Organs collectively make up an organism, such as a person or other animal. Each may have a central decision department or headquarters, or it may be a federated organization. Many human organs have departmental intelligence. The stomach, for example, is not just in charge of digestion. It has functions that can be compared to the cash flow manager of a corporation. Sufficient energy must be ensured for the overall body's functioning. If insufficient fuel is taken in to support it, a message must be sent to headquarters (the brain) that more fuel is needed. This is the feeling of hunger; it sometimes includes a headache or weakness or other signs. In case of excess food intake, safety deposits are made that will be used in times of fuel shortages. The complex management of demand created by energy and supply is remarkable. It gets even more complex when the brain decides that someone must diet to reduce excess energy savings in the form of fat.

As we begin to understand information flow in human bodies, the question of animal intelligence arises. It may take decades to understand most animal communication methods and languages, but there is progress in the study of cognitive ability in several species. Studies of dogs, chimpanzees, bonobos, dolphins, and elephants demonstrate their ability to capture and process information. Parrots, ravens, and other birds are also being studied. Many animals have better sensory capabilities than humans to capture information. Elephants, dogs, and other animals have a keener sense of smell. Birds have better vision. Consider a flock of birds trying to imagine the intelligence of a human person. The human may be able to recognize potential dangers through a thought process, but, from a bird's perspective, human vision is substandard. The bird, if it were capable of judging human intelligence, thus might find us sorely lacking. A comparison of the memory capacity of some animals and that of humans *without the artificial help of books or documents* might lead one to judge some aspects of human intelligence as underdeveloped.

People have always wondered about the intelligence of other living beings. Those who lived with animals sensed that their geese, horses, cats, or dogs had some kind of intelligence. Attempts to measure animal intelligence have persisted for centuries. The best-documented case occurred in Germany at the beginning of the twentieth. Wilhelm von Osten was so successful at teaching children that he decided to try his skills on animals. After teaching two horses, he boasted that one of them (who was famously known as *Clever Hans*), had been taught to do information processing the human way. He could even do mathematics and read. Despite the horse's lack of hands for writing, it was claimed he could add, subtract, multiply, divide, work with fractions, tell time, keep track of the calendar, and even read, spell and understand German. Indeed, the teacher demonstrated this before an independent board of thirteen specialists: the horse tapped his hoof or shook his head to provide mostly correct answers to many questions. Amazed by the presentations, the board ruled in September 1904 that "no tricks were involved" in the performance. It was official: *Clever Hans* could perform basic human information processing functions. However, because suspicion remained, further trials were done with questioners other than the horse's master without spectators. The horse still responded mostly with correct answers. Finally, the mystery was solved. The horse only got the questions right when the questioner knew the answer and the horse could see him. In other words, the horse had "body recognition software" that read communication in postural changes, facial expressions, and increased or decreased tension in the questioner. As anybody who lives with a domestic animal knows, this is similar to the way a dog or cat senses its master's departure, stress, or other state of mind that affects the owner's behavior. Many animals have an intelligence based on sensing intent from observed behavior.

Most people have some of these skills; it is more developed in some than others. A psychic or fortuneteller may have skills to make reasonable deductions from observations of the client's behavior. There are physicians who report that they sometimes learn more about a patient within the first ten seconds of interaction than from the details of the patient history.

So, do animals have intelligence? Does your dog have knowledge? The answer is yes, although neither animal intelligence in general, nor your dog's knowledge in particular, can be compared to human intelligence or knowledge. But what about ants and bees, who seem to have a higher level of social community than other beings? In their book on the superorganism of insects, Bert Hölldobler and E. O. Wilson claim that "Today, possibly half the species remain undiscovered, and of those given a scientific name, only a tiny fraction—1 percent or fewer—have been examined."[39] The authors found that colonies of insects are divided into castes: some reproductive, some working, some defending or fighting. The "superorganism" determines to what caste any member belongs. Collectively, they grow food and even have slaves. For a long time, insects were believed not to have intelligence. However, this view is changing as we learn more. Insects decide on issues as a group, such as moving on or preparing for an attack. Approximately 90 percent of the communication is chemical; the remainder is behavioral and to the human eye looks like a dance. Distinct algorithms have been identified that involve basic information processing resulting in communication. An ant can identify an object and determine whether it is friend or foe, and it can tell others in which direction food is and how far. These insects accept their places in the colony, and there is no sign of "free will." Each colony is like an organ with the intelligence of cells.

How does this relate to human societies? Think of the attempts at social engineering during the twentieth century. Whether in East European communism or in China, the attempt was made to test each child to determine a designated place in society for which it would be trained, with no less and no more information than required. The rapid developments in identifying people's knowledge skills might lead to the temptation to create superorganisms of humans. A group of children might be tested, their DNA determined, their intelligence levels assessed, and their schooling adjusted to fit each into a predetermined collective similar to a superorganism. In such a society, people might be assigned specific roles according to biological and intellectual capacity, their knowledge and decision making guided by "society counselors." Some people might call this a

---

39   Bert Hölldobler and E O Wilson, *The Superorganism: The Beauty, Elegance and Strangeness of Insect Societies.* (New York: W. W. Norton & Company, 2009), 12.

caste system, while others may see it as meaningful placement within an information society. It is important to understand the potential dangers of this form of information society and to protect against a slide into such a predesigned, networked superorganism.

Plants also acquire information—about environmental conditions, particularly sunlight, the essential fuel for many plants. What makes a plant turn toward light to seek better conditions? Is it similar to the body message that people experience as pleasure or pain? Plants definitely have some form of information capture and possibly very basic information processing as well as memory. As with cells and organs, plant "intelligence" cannot be measured against human intelligence, but it has certain strengths and weaknesses arising from survival needs. If information is the key element for living beings, from enzymes to viruses, from cells to interactive organs, from plants to animals to humans, what about the macrocosm, the universe, or even the multiverse?

Perhaps the best example of human chauvinism is our communication outreach into space. Considering the vastness of space and the number of stars, planets, and moons, it is probable that there is intelligent life somewhere within the 80 billion galaxies containing almost 100 sextillion stars (or triple that number, according to 2010 research[40]). And, most likely, this is not the last expansion of our limited understanding of the extent of our universe and the multiverse. If there are "intelligent beings" out there, then it is important to acknowledge that they may not communicate with sounds created in a larynx. They may have other communication systems. Just over a hundred years ago, a person could not imagine that in 2010, several billion people would receive their information over the air and through handheld devices connecting them worldwide. Past generations would marvel at the unprecedented effects on humanity. Why not accept that other forms of life may exist somewhere beyond this planet, with quite possibly more advanced intelligence than humans, who have different forms of communication and intelligence?

---

40   Pieter G van Dokkum and Charlie Conroy, "A substantial population of low-mass stars in luminous galaxies," *Nature*, December 16, 2010, 940–942.

The Ecosystem of Intelligence

Information is a key ingredient of any ecosystem. The hierarchy of ecosystems starts with the interaction within cells and proceeds to the ecosystem of this planet (and beyond). Each participant has its own intelligence, yet driven by the same motivators as its peers; e.g., finding fuel, surviving, reproducing, and so on. In other words, each participant in an ecosystem has only the intellectual capacity needed for survival within that ecosystem. In decision making, each being searches for a solution in order to thrive. This means that intelligence is based on solutions that come from problem solving. When animals die, those that survive may learn something to survive. If a medication fights a virus, the virus has to learn how to adjust or get stronger if it is to survive. It is important to consider the intelligence of living matter on this planet when making environmental decisions. After all, intelligence and energy make the world tick. People may finally begin to fully understand the information storage and processing capabilities of all living beings in the twenty-first century.

Human vs. WIC Intelligence

Several issues will come to the forefront as WIC expands and becomes more powerful. Most changes will come from two factors. The first is because WIC's knowledge base is estimated to be millions of times bigger than the memory capacity of any person. Consider all the knowledge in all the languages of the planet plus the more than 100 million books that are being made available through digitizing. This almost unimaginable expansion of knowledge prompts the following questions: What information does a person have to learn to be most proficient and effective in professional and personal information management? What information must be learned in order to make the best use of WIC?

The second major factor is an increasing understanding of the brain's strengths and weaknesses versus those of WIC. The brain's memory is selective and limited by pattern recognition. Often, we see what we want to see and hear what we want to hear. Information processing is subject to the influence of human software motivators, such as anger, revenge, sex drive, or other competitive drives. Most of all, the brain tends to place data and information within a context—a belief system. In other words, people try to make sense of information by comparing it with their belief systems. The combination of human motivators and creative problem-solving algorithms has distinct advantages over artificial intelligence and its predictable logic. The brain assembles data from memory and integrates them with new information that leads to creativity and problem solving. Consider storytelling: Before the mainstream use of books, storytellers made their living creating fascinating stories. From there, others added images and embellishments. For the most part, books have replaced storytelling, yet they too stimulate creative thinking. Artificial intelligence projects have made the first attempts to have computers create stories, but it remains to be seen whether artificial intelligence can match the mind's creativity in any way. After all, it is the human brain that creates computers, programs them, and gives them the ability to solve problems. The brain is truly the mind behind the machine.

Any company that outsources services or manufacturing knows that there comes a point where a subcontractor has learned enough to become a competitor. This is an inevitable development. Is the same possible in the computer/human partnership? The wealth of information on the WIC may be viewed today as a useful tool or even as a form of subcontracting. With the increase in machine learning and the rise in artificial intelligence, we have to ask ourselves: What will become of the WIC-brain partnership?

While it is difficult to foresee all changes in human intelligence, here are ten major possibilities to consider:

1. *A shift from memorizing to information navigation and conceptual understanding.* The shift from brain-centric information systems to WIC-centric information systems requires new intelligence structures. These will demand appropriate knowledge of an information field in order to connect its dots. For instance, the traditional learning of historical

data is less important than understanding historical *concepts.* Educational authorities need to reexamine what basic knowledge is required to understand concepts in any particular knowledge field.

2. *Online and virtual learning as a new educational paradigm.* This will lead to less emphasis on traditional educational degrees and standardized knowledge levels. Slowly, perhaps over thirty years or so, new ways of education will evolve as classroom teaching gives way to personal coaching and self-guided learning. Much necessary core knowledge will be recorded and reused, but in widely divergent and creative ways. Indeed, creativity in capturing and keeping student interest will be the key to successful teaching software. Multiple ways—perhaps hundreds—will develop to teach the same material, adjusted to a student's language, current knowledge inventory, interests, capacity, customs, culture, and/or special needs. Much of the learning process will be in the form of games that will stimulate students to learn. At the same time, a new industry will evolve that will develop teaching materials for anyone with any disability or anyone in remote sites who cannot go to traditional schools. The traditional structures of high school or college diplomas will diminish. For instance, the treatise that in the past only a PhD student could research and write can already be achieved by a person with less formal training but sufficient interest and intellect, combined with research opportunities. The implications of these dramatic changes may not yet be fully understood or anticipated by educational institutions from preschools to postgraduate schools and universities.

3. *A new relationship between accessible knowledge and concept knowledge.* People's intelligence will change under WIC. The mind will have to learn to react faster and achieve a higher level of alertness. People will have to learn how to manage and adjust to digital devices, skills not needed in the past. Children are learning these skills through some digital games. In years to come, a large percentage of people will be monitoring computer systems in much the same way that pilots now monitor

in-flight computers. Time management will also be important. Turning off "digital information partners" such as computers, mobile phones, and other devices will be limited to sleeping hours and special circumstances. Just as our ancestors roaming through the wilderness several thousand years ago had to be alert all the time to protect themselves from predators, it will become necessary for people to be alert to opportunities and threats communicated via digital devices.

4. *New WIC literacy.* There will be several levels of WIC literacy. At the highest level, it will combine reading, writing, and math skills with value knowledge (professional and cultural vs. trivial), supplemented by a deep computer understanding and the ability to write software and create apps for mobile devices, as well as to design and modify games to one's liking. WIC literacy leads to WIC intelligence, including setting a personally acceptable level of privacy and security as well as skills to distinguish facts from spin. Other levels of WIC literacy will enable people in less developed countries to connect to WIC and acquire knowledge for better living in their language and according to their culture. In other words, people in remote villages will be able to learn how to be self-sufficient, grow enough food, research, teach, and so on through WIC communication in their own language. WIC will become accessible worldwide, enabling WIC literacy even in remote areas that do not now have connectivity.

5. *Transition from linear book reading to multimedia information capture.* What began in comic books (images with action text) is likely to develop into a new form of reading involving more senses. This will top three-dimensional movie experiences. In content organization, fiction books will not likely change much, since they follow the storytelling feature of the brain, but they will be further enhanced by images and perhaps sounds and smells as well. However, nonfiction books will likely change from demanding linear pattern recognition for reading long passages to offering shorter messages that include images and other sensory enhancements. The focus will be on organizing and indexing information for easy

capture and understanding. Books as we now know them may be rare.

6. *Mobile devices/apps as digital companions.* The development of apps on mobile phones and tablets is a relatively new phenomenon. With such apps, mobile phones are becoming digital companions, assisting people personally and professionally. These digital companions provide knowledge, practical guidance, and entertainment, as they integrate functions previously dispersed in our lives: watch, alarm clock, book and music library, teaching tool, communication device, etc. With WIC, the digital companion will change our daily lives.

7. *The shift from productivity to creativity.* In WIC, automation will take over more industries, and computers will produce more goods and facilitate the delivery of more services, reducing the traditional workforce. Consequently, the focus of intelligence in WIC will change from productivity to new ideas and creative solutions at all levels: personal, organizational, governmental, and global.

8. *WIC-based fact-checking becomes routine.* The human mind has a tendency to subordinate facts to belief systems. As a result, truth is often bent to promote, support, or justify beliefs. Such twisting of truth can be found in all human communications. WIC allows automated fact-checking. A new profession of fact-checkers will evolve, and software developers will produce fact-checking apps that anyone can use.

9. *The move to transparency and knowledge equality.* The concept of freedom has long been a major motivator, particularly in the European and North American world. Transparency is the freedom to know an organization's reasons and motivators for actions and information processing. Keeping information secret is the opposite of informational freedom. WIC requires that the ideal of freedom be applied to information and knowledge systems. Knowledge equality will also affect global intelligence systems. All people should have the same ability to acquire WIC knowledge, independent of language, cultural constraints, personal interests, information processing capabilities, social status, and financial situation.

10. *The brain's new role in dominating the information field.* WIC is still in an embryonic state. As systems grow and become more powerful through machine learning and artificial intelligence, real competition will develop between WIC and the brain. Early simple competition in chess or TV trivia games has shown the capability of properly programmed search engines. The brain will be challenged to maximize its partnership with WIC to advance ourselves and our world beyond what our brains can accomplish outside that partnership.

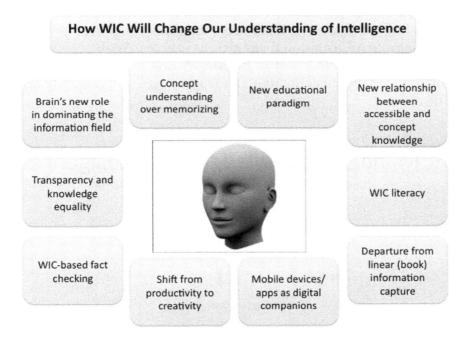

Figure 3. How WIC will change our understanding of intelligence

Four Levels of Intelligence

As intelligence and knowledge management change, new understandings of them are needed. At the lowest level of intelligence, data are converted into information. This occurs biologically when our eyes see shades of light or when we create words out of characters. The result is perceived information. (Whether what is perceived is actually true has been a subject of debate for thousands of years.) The second level of intelligence is the sophisticated process of making sense of bits of information. Context is analyzed to fit the information into a wider scenario. In many cases, this process involves the attempt to fit the information into an appropriate belief system. If the information fits our belief system or is believed to be authentic, then it is accepted as knowledge. The third level is complex computing with systems whose data processing power exceeds that of the brain. At this level, a great deal of information is being processed within WIC. The fourth level is analytic intelligence: the ability to extract, analyze, and integrate information from various sources. Analytics is applied not only by individuals but in businesses and enterprises, where it provides valuable insights that can lead to greater competitiveness and success.

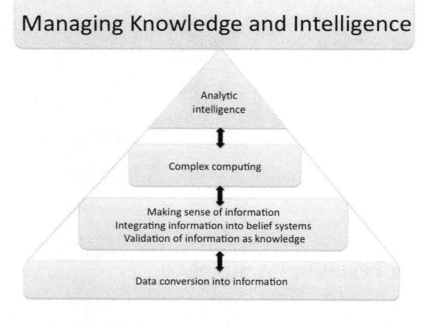

Figure 4. Managing knowledge and intelligence

Business Intelligence and Enterprise Intelligence

Each of our many personal intelligence systems is based on specific knowledge and appropriate information processing. Similarly, organizations need to interlink specific knowledge fields, mine their data, and extract contextualized value. While business intelligence addresses the extraction of valuable data from various business fields, enterprise intelligence addresses overall enterprise information management. Both enterprise intelligence and business intelligence are part of an organization's knowledge capital management.

Organizations have begun to understand the value of enterprise intelligence, which aims to connect the dots between data silos in an organization to discover information that is valuable for decision making. Several companies offer analytics software that does typical intelligence operations: collecting and analyzing data from several sources to improve cost control, operations, predictive trends, quality assurance, productivity, streamlined administrative operations, and other processes.

More refinement in these approaches to managing information will appear in the next decade. They will provide increased knowledge about an organization's knowledge strength, departmental and functional intelligence, and competitive (or market) intelligence, and the environment that affects business (laws, rules, opportunities, and so on).

Intelligence Is Everywhere

All living beings have intelligence. But how does that account for higher intelligence—more than is needed to simply live and survive—particularly in humans? Enter one of the principles of life: challenge and response. When challenged, a living being may reach beyond its standard intelligence level and advance its information processing capabilities. A business may respond similarly when challenged. The acquisition of further knowledge and higher information processing capabilities follows the development of more complex life forms and organizations. In these processes, knowledge capital is the key ingredient.

4

Human Software

Whereas most knowledge used to be accessible only through educational institutions, books, library material, magazines, newspapers, and mass media, today knowledge can expand with research and access to information in WIC. If the interest and will exist, an information seeker can satisfy the hunger for knowledge according to interest and information acquisition and processing capabilities. In this process it is important to make the difficult distinction between accurate and inaccurate information. While many take widespread belief in a piece of information as validation of its accuracy, there are endless examples of accepted beliefs that were later proven incorrect. Governments intentionally distribute misinformation, as do some corporations and other organizations. There was a time when certain authorities could claim that their information was more valid than others', but democratic information developments are changing the automatic assumption that traditional authorities provide accurate information

The human processing system's ability to put data into context is complex. Imagine seeing a small part of a picture. In order to make sense of it, one must see a larger part, or even the complete picture. Similarly, when the brain receives a message, it must try to figure out its relationship to other data. The brain tries "to get the picture," as the saying goes. Every person acquires many belief systems in a lifetime. Our minds constantly determine whether information is true, correct, or plausible, as they test whether the incoming information fits into our belief systems. If information can be validated within the belief system, the information is accepted. If it does not fit, we determine that the information is wrong, incorrect, and/or implausible. If the information refers to a new subject, a new belief system may be created. The resulting interpretation may or may not conform to the facts, but it also includes prejudices and opinions, as well as various sets of knowledge and information theories.

There is a difference between communicating incorrect information that is believed to be correct within a belief systems and the purposeful distribution of incorrect information. Disinformation is designed, for instance, by politicians or governments to purposefully mislead people. This raises the question, "Which information can one trust?" Because there is a potential gap between "official information" and accurate information from corporations, organizations, and government, each person must decide whom and what to believe. This is part of knowledge capital management. The traditional acceptance of information generated by governments may need to be cautioned against as we become more aware of how information can be influenced and distorted. Every person manipulates information every day, whether for self or others. While most of our tweaking of information is unnoticed and much of it is done unconsciously, the observer must be alert to extreme manipulation—for instance, politically biased content in newspapers, radio stations, TV stations, cable channels, and so on. Bits of such information are based on facts, but the content expressed through specific belief systems is usually very different. A person must be selective about information sources and should stay open to opposing or alternative views. While the question of which information one can trust is very old, the skill to detect what is accurate, misleading, and inaccurate is becoming increasingly important. Our perceptions constantly adjust realities to belief systems. Multiple intelligences, as described in the previous chapter, interact with our belief systems and influence our information processing capabilities. In other words, our data acquisition processes provide information that is then adjusted or manipulated to fit into our belief systems.

But what goes on during human information processing? What causes our decision making process to malfunction? Why do people knowingly break the law? Why do people do things that don't make sense to others? Why does someone procrastinate some work items but is energized by others? In other words, what makes us tick?

The complex system of human information processing has several components. The first is biological memory. DNA, for example, provides us with many algorithms for life decisions, but early forecasts that DNA information might provide insights about future character traits, personal preferences, lifestyles, or decisions were too optimistic. Are we really programmed for most of the decisions we make and actions we take? For some time, the debate centered on the degree to which our actions are programmed by nature and to what degree they are subject to influences leading to new reasoning and decisions. Evelyn Fox Keller compares the degree of biological inheritance from our genes with how we are shaped by life experiences.[41] Philosophers and others have long developed ideologies that explain human information processing principles.

At the end of the nineteenth century, Sigmund Freud published his theories on the unconscious mind, focusing on the unconscious part of decision making. His theories were widely adopted and well accepted at the time, and psychoanalysis was a popular way to look at human motivation. However, the rational identification of unconscious motives has not always led to changes in them: the client on the psychiatrist's couch does not necessarily change his obsessions or unethical behavior as a result of discussing them rationally. Freud's theories fell from general acceptance at the beginning of the twentieth century to general skepticism, if not rejection, by its end. Science had changed its focus from the subjective psychological approach to a neurological approach that attempted to explain the brain's "hardware issues." Nevertheless,

---

41   Evelyn Fox Keller, *The Mirage of a Space Between Nature and Nurture* (Durham: Duke University Press, 2010).

the idea that emotions must be studied to understand human information processing keeps returning. Abraham Maslow developed a theory of a "hierarchy of needs" in the 1950s to describe his concept of self-actualization. Robert Plutchik has identified more than ninety emotions and an equal number of theories.[42] Emotions are not just feelings, but information processes that involve cognition, particularly perception and pattern recognition, as well as context and belief system assignment. To understand human motivations, it is important to discuss ingrained human algorithms, because in the future the brain will have to work with WIC networks that provide artificial intelligence, an immense knowledge resource, and powerful information processing.

Human Motivators

Human thinking includes data acquisition and biological memory, as well as several kinds of motivators that process information according to biologically ingrained "software." Consider each of these motivators as an algorithm that springs into place when a certain situation arises. Emotions are a kind of human software that makes people react. For instance, when a person feels slighted, the software stimulates the emotional motivator for anger. The cause may be a minor mental pain the person may not be fully conscious of. Similarly, other feelings may stimulate specific reactions.

The most basic motivators of human behavior are pain and the seeking of joy and pleasure. Although we are motivated by joy and pleasure, the result is often short-lived. Pleasure is subjective; it is influenced by culture and many other factors.

The complex internal communication system between organs and body parts is not yet sufficiently understood. Biological communication includes the conscious and unconscious management of body parts. When you want to lift an arm, walk, raise your head, type on a keyboard, play a ball game, jump, stretch, climb, or do any

---

42   Robert Plutchik, "The Nature of Emotions," *American Scientist*, July-August 2001, 344.

other activity with complex body movements, the body must issue commands to coordinate movement. Biological malfunctions are expressed as pain, a kind of alarm system that alerts us that something is wrong. Compare this to a light or sound in a car that alerts the driver to a malfunction.

The body information management system is a kind of building block of biological intelligence. Eyes, nose, ears, skin, taste buds, skin, and other data acquisition systems also manage data input through our senses. Our pattern recognition "software" and mental activity require substantial intelligence. The body information management system is therefore an essential gateway to the human information system. Perception, imagination, memory, and emotion and other information processes are part of the human central information processing and storage unit, the mind, which coordinates the biological memory of basic algorithms our ancestors acquired long ago. It also processes ancient motivators that function like human software to lead us to react in specific life situations according to established rules.

There are three kinds of human motivators. *Life motivators* are shared by most living beings. They represent the core algorithms for life: survival, food sustenance, and reproduction. *Emotional motivators* have been evolving for thousands of years: They affect energy levels and catalyze action (out of love, anger, or other feeling). But to live together in civilization, people had to be taught how to behave. These algorithms, first developed in individual, tribe-like settings and later refined in religious beliefs and through social ethics, constitute *learned motivators*. In general terms, the mind serves as the overall information acquisition, processing and storage facility. The brain and environment interact and produce an unconscious response to what is going on around us. Perception, assumptions, expectations, and other forms of information processing are part of the mind. These stored algorithms govern processes that lead to moral intentions, ethical and unethical thinking and behavior, as well as the formation of belief systems. A very large part of our daily functioning is influenced and governed by these mental processes.

What People and Animals Have In Common: Life Motivators

Life motivators are the strongest biological memory algorithms. These are the biological building blocks of living beings, but we are not certain how they developed. The drive for survival—the desire to live—keeps a person going even if circumstances are very painful. On the rare occasion when this motivator is corrupted, suicide can result.

Closely linked to the drive for survival is the life motivator algorithm that makes beings protect themselves. In our modern society, open attacks are generally unlikely, but the strong intuitive sense that identifies potential enemies may lead one to dislike or feel hostile toward a colleague, for instance, because of the unconscious perception of a threat. Fear is part of this motivator and affects many functions in animals and people. Fear can empower a person to fight or flee, but it also can cause immobility if it leads to fatalism and acceptance of a threatening situation.

Sustenance is another life motivator. When someone is hungry and has no resources to get food, this module drives the overcoming of constraints to find fuel.

Finally, there is the life motivator for reproduction, expressed as a desire for sex. Have you wondered why powerful people, particularly politicians, are willing to risk their families, honor, dignity, and power for an affair or sexual incident? The basic sex drive may override morals or learned discipline when given the opportunity.

Living beings are subject to a wide range of other biological software applications. It would exceed the scope of this book to examine them all, but let me just briefly mention some. There is a general attraction to beauty. Further, living beings (and even companies and organizations) create more energy when they are challenged. In horse races or similar competitive events, animals run faster because others are competing. People enjoy competitions, for instance, in games. In contrast, there is also a drive to conform and assimilate in the presence of others. Many animals, but particularly humans, desire freedom. We also need to be loved and to create harmony. People also have a desire for success (and, once achieved, for further success).

Figure 5. Life motivators are prime motivators, which humans have in common with animals and other living beings. We are programmed to want to live (except in rare cases of suicide), to protect ourselves, to sustain the body with food and nourishment, and to replicate (sex drive).

Life motivators are basic human software modules that work in the background and kick in when an occasion arises. They may compete with other motivators for dominance during information processing. Their strength is particularly influenced by the second type of human software: the emotional ecosystem.

Emotional Motivators

Our human software includes emotional motivators (EMs). An emotion can be described as the "complex psychophysiological experience of an individual's state of mind as interacting with biochemical (internal) and environmental (external) influences."[43] In other words, an emotion is not a feeling, but a piece of software that runs according to specific algorithms. The key ingredients are perceived information that causes a specific feeling and information-processing algorithms that interpret it. Emotional motivators produce good or bad, sad or joyful, angry or trusting, loving or hating, hopeful or disappointed feelings. They cause us to feel as if we like or dislike something, including everyone we meet.

---

43   Wikipedia: http://en.wikipedia.org/wiki/Emotion.

According to this basic decision process, behavior is friendly or unfriendly, with a range of options between the two extremes. Such behavior often cannot be explained rationally, but it influences many human interactions.

EMs have evolved over thousands of years. They traditionally represent the tip of the iceberg of feelings and motivations that govern behavior. To emote is to display exaggerated emotion, to limit one's openness, and to be subject to a strong motivation. Often, someone showing a strong emotion may not be willing to listen to reason. In many cases, this results in a more strident and forceful expression of the emotion. But emotions are not limited to rare instances of exaggerated behavior. They influence or govern the decision making and thinking processes of our daily lives. They are information processes that motivate a person when a specific set of feelings are experienced. People are often not aware of their emotional motivators because they (and those around them) recognize the motivator only when it is exaggerated. Of course, EMs are linked to—and both influence and are influenced by—the life motivators described above. Feelings are determined by the strength of the emotional motivator being experienced.

The most important and influential EM is the unconscious desire to "feel good." Feeling good is connected to (or can be produced by) other EMs— for example, success or being loved. It can also be inverted into depression or feeling horrible. There is a scale of feeling great, feeling ok, and at the bottom of the scale, feeling terrible or depressed. When we achieve financial success in business or win the lottery, the special good feeling fades quickly, leading one to strive for more and continue to succeed. Being in love makes you feel good, but this also fades with time. Humans have sought artificial ways to feel good for thousands of years. Alcohol consumption and psychoactive drugs have been traditional mood elevators, but they too are temporary. Another alternative is information therapy, including daydreaming, meditation, and yoga, combined with a will for change.

Emotional Motivators

Affection	Desire	Hatred	Joy	Regret
Anger	Despair	Hope	Liking	Remorse
Angst	Disappointment	Horror	Loathing	Sadness
Annoyance	Disgust	Hostility	Loneliness	Satisfaction
Anxiety	Disliking	Hysteria	Love	Shame
Apathy	Dread	Indifference	Lust	Shock
Arousal	Ecstasy	Expectations	Misery	Shyness
Awe	Embarrassment	Fear	Obsession	Sorrow
Boldness	Envy	Fearlessness	Panic	Suffering
Boredom	Euphoria	Frustration	Passion	Surprise
Contempt	Excitement	Gratitude	Pity	Terror
Contentment	Expectations	Grief	Pleasure	Wonder
Curiosity	Guilt	Interest	Pride	Worry
Depression	Happiness	Jealousy	Rage	

Figure 6. Emotional motivators

Learned Motivators

Learned motivators are a suite of human software painstakingly taught to children to transform them into civilized members of society. The purpose of these algorithms is to guide members within communities, provide protocols for behavior, instill (religious and community-developed) morals and values, and establish guidelines for living in a community. Societal values and literacy are key information-processing algorithms that are imprinted in children at an early age. The Christian Ten Commandments, the Jewish Torah, the Hindu Principles of Moral Thought and Action, and the Islamic Commandments with five obligatory duties, as well as laws related to alcohol, gambling, food, business, crime, and punishment, are all examples of such social and personal software algorithms. Most schools, parents, and others also teach children a wide range of other human software belief systems. They teach values for living together, ethical concerns, personal and professional skills, and knowledge management. Some modules include rules for collaboration, concern for and respect for others, equality, fairness, personal discipline, neighborliness, and service to society.

It is easy to forget that these rules are superimposed on basic animalistic software. Conflicts between these can lead to unethical behavior and crime. Many are challenged with the struggle between the stronger life software that was installed, say, thirty thousand years ago, and the disciplinary software that they were taught as children and afterward. For example, millions of stockholders are tempted to demand maximum investment returns without considering whether a company pays its share in taxes, employs child labor indirectly, or engages in other unacceptable or unethical business practices. The important point is that these behaviors are not governed by DNA or other biological knowledge, but rather are the outcome of the struggle between information processes and motivators.

Learned Motivators

- Religious beliefs
- Social values and behavior
- Mathematics and logical deductions
- Literacy (reading, writing, WIC literacy)
- Discipline: Law abidance, self-control, conforming to societal expectations, etc.
- Human base knowledge
- Culture and arts
- Framework of skills
- Integrity
- Others

Figure 7. Learned motivators

The resolution of conflict among these three groups of motivators is the basis for human information processing and behavior.

Three Phases of Processing in Our Mind

The graphic below illustrates the three phases of information processing. The body information system (upper left area in the illustration) includes information captured by our five senses, intuition, and bio-messages (from DNA to cell communication), as well as pain messages. In the first phase, pattern recognition processes all captured information, establishes context, and makes sense of the incoming messages. The central component (second phase) is the information storage and processing system, where three categories of motivators are often in conflict and challenge each other. This challenge is responded to by drawing information from memory, and the winning motivator (or combination of motivators) leads to decisions, which are influenced by belief systems. In the third phase, a process of internal review and reconciliation takes place, both consciously and unconsciously (often while sleeping), resulting in belief system integration. Consider knee-jerk reactions that your conscious brain would like to rework later. Or consider the old rule of "sleeping on" options before making a decision, giving the information processing system a chance to review options and their consequences. Now, let's move on to discuss the essential EM: a desire for well-being.

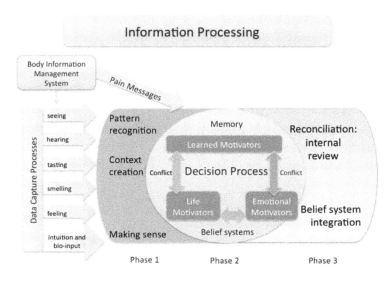

Figure 8. Information processing

Well-being

Many emotional motivators are linked to a universal theme: People are driven by a desire for happiness and "feeling good." While the feeling of happiness usually does not last, we've made some progress toward understanding what gives people a general sense of well-being, and there are efforts to measure the happiness of people in different places. Scales for measuring well-being range from happiness to unhappiness and from good feelings to bad. Feeling good or bad depends on momentary experiences, each assigned a relative value on the good/bad dimension.[44] Much of this judgment is subjective and based on how satisfied with life people are at the time.

One study found that four major factors contribute to how moods are categorized. They include the *general* state (41 to 53 percent), *expectations* (22 to 40 percent), *past events* (5 to 20 percent), and *social comparison* (5 to 13 percent).[45] The *general* mood might be influenced by such things as an argument with friends or family, political information that does not fit into a belief system, or dissatisfaction with work. *Expectations,* directly linked to hope, are connected with an emotional motivator that can make a person feel better or worse and get more or less inner energy. *Past events* may cause good or bad feelings that persist. *Social comparison* is the motivator that a person uses to measure the self against neighbors, colleagues, neighborhoods, and even other countries; it produces a feeling on the scale of good to bad. For instance, if a neighbor is perceived to be able to afford more luxury goods, one's own feeling of well-being may go down a couple of notches.

The key effect of EMs is the distribution of body energy. The higher the feeling is on the "good" scale, the more energy is generated by the information system. The EMs of rage and anger provide

---

44   Daniel Kahneman, "Objective Happiness," *Well Being: The Foundations of Hedonic Psychology*, ed. Daniel Kahneman, Ed Diener and Norbert Schwarz (New York, Russell Sage Foundation, 1999), 7.

45   Norbert Schwarz and Fritz Strack, "Reports of Subjective Well-Being: Judgmental Processes and Their Methodological Implications," *Well Being: The Foundations of Hedonic Psychology*, ed. Daniel Kahneman, Ed Diener, and Norbert Schwarz (New York, Russell Sage Foundation, 1999), 61.

extra energy for attacking the target of the feeling. The EM of revenge is considered acceptable in some religions. This information-processing algorithm, where violence is applied as a response to violence, is an example that might have been appropriate thousands of years ago but does not incorporate modern thought processes for conflict resolution. The same applies to the EM of "doing justice." "Justice" is a subjective concept that many countries and cultures interpret differently. One wonders: Will globalization bring a more global understanding of it?

Changing EMs

As noted, EMs may be in conflict with the algorithms for information processing and behavior that we teach to children. Does that mean that humans are stuck with EMs that can be destructive and cause unnecessary violence? There is evidence that EMs can change as cultures change, establishing new customs and preferred behaviors. Consider the EM of honor, which can mean something like "principled uprightness of character and personal integrity." From the eleventh to the twentieth century, any perceived insult would violate someone's honor. The EM honor algorithm demanded that the violation be avenged by a duel, a prearranged combat between two persons using deadly weapons. Although exact numbers are hard to come by, it is reported that during the eighteen years of Henry IV's reign, approximately four thousand people were killed in duels.[46] Today, dueling is generally outlawed or has become a "mock" duel conducted with nonlethal weapons.

Another example of a changing EM is the concern for people who are physically, cognitively, mentally, or otherwise challenged. Disabled people were not a target of empathy and caring until the late twentieth century. Attitudes have changed, and our society has a very different EM in this regard. This may signal that other EMs can be changed, particularly those resulting in violence, ("an eye for an eye"), as well as those that motivate war. Will future EMs motivate voters to elect politicians who are experts in conflict resolution?

---

46 http://Wikisource.org/The New International Encyclopedia/Dueling.

Future Human Software Developments

Knowledge developments are moving toward knowledge expansion and more transparency, both in their decision making processes and their consequences. In the future, a digital companion might notify someone that he or she is acting inappropriately and that it may be time to take a more rational approach. The reader who thinks that this is unrealistic should be reminded that Grandma could never have imagined that a computer-generated voice would be telling her how to find her way from one place to another. The algorithms for reacting to a specific event depend on the values and processes stored in a person's mind. The sum of algorithms makes up one's character: the "complex of mental and ethical traits marking and often individualizing a person, group or nation."[47] It used to be assumed that this combination of acquired ethical rules and algorithms would stay constant—that one's character was firmly established by a combination of hereditary values and disciplined upbringing. A villain would always be expected to act like a villain, and a gentleman would be expected to continue to act like a gentleman. In fact, intellectual responses to challenges are fluid. Traits can and may change when challenged. That is, behavioral patterns can be changed with an understanding of the information processes of EM systems within value systems.

To sum up, human information processing represents a complex set of software—some learned, some inherited; these are constantly challenged by emotional motivators. As people live within WIC, they will be challenged by its logical algorithms. The information in WIC already far exceeds what any human brain can hold; the brain must yield to the superior storage capabilities of WIC. WIC's artificial computing processes will show people where emotional processing is leading them astray. Decision makers may act less out of anger, revenge, power, and political opportunity when WIC gives an enhanced awareness of violations of peace and ethical guidelines, as well as a cool estimate of the resulting cost in lives, resources, reputation, and future opportunities.

---

47   *Merriam-Webster Dictionary* http://www.merriam-webster.com/dictionary/character.

5

From Data and Knowledge
to Wisdom

Information management is a matter of life and death for living beings. Similarly, non-biological organizations such as corporations and governments succeed or fail according to their ability to manage information.

Information falls into five categories: data, information, belief systems, knowledge, and wisdom. Data are the units or symbols that form the basis of all information. Examples of data include computer bytes, pixels, sensations of light, the softness of an object, a scent, a sound, etc. Living beings capture data through senses and use algorithms to make sense of them. At the technical level (when machines and devices are used), data capture involves methods of recording and deciphering data, such as handwriting, listening to dictation and/or transcribing it, keying or otherwise inputting data into a computer. Data are increasingly captured by devices from devices (called machine to machine or M2M). For other beings such as bees or ants, data may be detected chemically or behaviorally.

How information is captured, that is, which system is used to connect the dots, influences the outcome. This is true for the simplest activities as well as the most profound, such as whether to attack or be friendly. Just as energy sources come in many forms, information is created from data that exist in many forms.

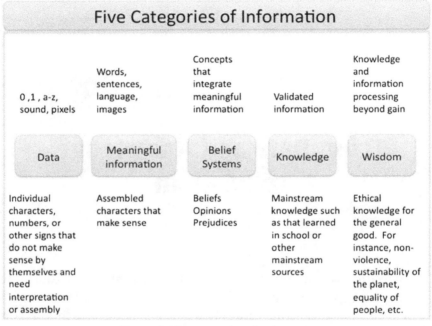

Figure 9. Five categories of information

From Data to Information

Data are information elements, each of which is without context or meaning when viewed in isolation. A character is a data element, as is a number or a binary digit. A single data element, or even a group of data elements, does not allow us to make sense of an object. Algorithms, rules, and guidance in the form of brain intelligence are needed to determine meaning. The ability to identify space in three dimensions and to make sense of a room or an area is not coded at birth, as one might assume. People who have been born blind and gain sight through an operation must learn this capability.[48] Further, while learning about space and object size occurs at a very early age, other algorithms are needed for putting these data into context. In early childhood, we also learn how to convert environmental and emotional data into context and to form rules. Consider what happens when one reads. First, the data must be captured. Neuroscientist Stanislas Dehene says that we do not scan the text as we read. Instead, our eyes identify ten to twelve letters, fixate on three to four to the left of the group, and as many as seven or eight to the right. He argues that "every written word is probably encoded by a hierarchical tree in which letters are grouped into larger size units, which are themselves grouped into syllables and words—much as the human body can be represented as an arrangement of legs, arms, torso, and head, each of which can be further broken down into simple parts."[49] This process is the first step in making sense of data presented in writing. Reading problems signify that data are not being captured appropriately. This is just an example of the complex processes necessary to advance from data to meaningful information in the reading process. Similar complexity exists in the processes of hearing, smelling, and tasting, as well as in the sensation of nerve ends on our largest organ, the skin. And, not to be ignored, our intuitive sensory functions are even more complex. Through all of these processes, we create information from data. Similarly, in the computer world, data processing converts data into information through computational functions.

Data Capture: Documentation, Authentication, and Communication

The validity of information has always been a concern. The information in a document must not be altered if it is to maintain its integrity. Initially, this was usually guaranteed by using a medium,

---

48   Richard Held, et al., "The newly blind fail to match seen with felt," *Nature Neuroscience*, April 10, 2011, 14:551–553.

49   Stanislas Dehene, *Reading in the Brain: The New Science of How We Read* (Penguin Kindle Edition, 2010), location 392.

such as paper, that did not easily allow text alteration. Further, a ruler's or business executive's seal on the paper further indicated the integrity of the document. The signature is still recognized as the sign that a person takes full responsibility for a document's content.

As computers created information that was not in document form and could easily be altered, facsimile technology rapidly gained acceptance. The document could be scanned in its entirety and sent as digital data via telephone lines to a receiving machine that could print it out as an image. Faxing is still the preferred method of document communication among lawyers, physicians, and many corporations and professions. However, a document's integrity may be better preserved when it is saved in an unchangeable digital format (such as an image format) or in a word processing format, such as MS Word or Apple's Pages, that allows text to be locked. There is a danger of manipulation in faxing, because a part of the document can be covered up or sections replaced with other text. For the receiver to be confident of a facsimile's integrity, its sender should provide assurance that it is unchanged when compared to the original document.[50] It should be noted, too, that scanning a document and sending it as an email attachment raises the same concerns. Where integrity is important, this method, too, should require validation.

For thousands of years, documents have been the primary means of presenting data as information. Think of a letter with its standard components: heading, sender identification, date, addressee identification, opening greetings, main message, complimentary closing, and signature. Each component consists of a number of data elements. Together, they represent the total information communicated in the letter. Because our thinking has traditionally been document-centric, computerization initially meant simply recreating electronically the same documents that had been on paper; that is, presenting collective data in formats similar to those of the past. More recently, it has been recognized that it is simpler and more

---

50   C Peter Waegemann, *Handbook of Optical Memory Systems* (The Optical Disk Institute, 1990).

efficient to present data more systematically and to format those data into more traditional documents only if desired or required.

Authentication has been a major concern in this transition from old-fashioned letters and documents to computerized documents and computerized communications. Putting a signature to a letter or other document has traditionally identified the writer (or originator, if it was transcribed by someone else), signified that the writer/originator meant to communicate the message, and took responsibility for it. Paper documents also implied that the message had kept data integrity: it had not been altered in any way. With data-centric computers, special care must be taken to create a document that cannot be changed. The biggest problem is the computer signature, which has three functions. First, it identifies the author; second, it certifies that the author takes responsibility for the text; and third, it implies data integrity for the signed document. The identification component has traditionally been simple, since the legible or semi-legible signature is person-specific. It is very unlikely that someone else on this planet writes the signature "Peter Waegemann" just as I do, unless someone studies my signature and illegally copies it. Even then, signature experts could distinguish my valid signature from a forged one. But what do you do when you are on the internet? User identification on the internet has still not been fully resolved. Nevertheless, internet commerce has grown to trillions of dollars. Buyers use software-based identification, which usually involves a combination of person-specific information such as an email address, a mother's maiden name, name of first pet, name of a school, etc., plus specific demographic and/or credit card information. Most users seem to feel this works adequately.

Digital signatures were promoted in the early years of the twenty-first century. A complex system of private and public key authentication has not had the acceptance that some security experts predicted. Widespread adoption of satisfactory authentication requires both ease of use and stringent security measures. Banks are especially concerned about internet security. A person can do great damage by transferring huge sums of money under a false identity. Here the tension is substantial: The strong security measures adopted by European banks, for example, are difficult to use;

they tend to discourage internet banking. Systems must be developed that allow relatively easy but safe internet banking, including electronic payments, transfers, and other transactions, since their operational costs are lower than traditional check processing or other paper-based transactions, and they facilitate commerce anywhere, anytime. Finding the right balance between ease of use and security is the key. The move to increased camera use might lead to future identification through a picture taken at the terminal or with a mobile device. Location services that determine a person's location at the time of transaction will also help determine whether it is Peter Waegemann at his desk in Boston or it is someone else, somewhere else, who is trying to access money from his account. Biometric identification systems, based on face recognition, fingerprints, hand recognition, retina scans, and voice recognition have long held promise in helping identifying people automatically, yet they still have not been widely adopted.

In Europe, a smartcard-style passport with a computer chip has been introduced that can also be used as an internet identification device. It remains to be seen whether this government-issued identification will become widely used in European internet transactions. As new technologies rapidly emerge, any government plans are likely to become quickly outdated by commercial solutions that are easier to use and equally as safe—perhaps more so.

A tremendous evolution has taken place in the way data are used to compose letters, notes, manuscripts, and other documents. The typewriter became a businessperson's personal printing device, creating print-like characters and eliminating problems associated with reading handwriting. The electric typewriter of the 1960s was the first instrument to offer limited editing and correction capabilities. The revolution in print communication began with the introduction of stand-alone word processors, first introduced in the 1970s and 1980s. Considered in their early days as a way to prepare official documents, word processors offered an easy way to compose text, edit, and format it. As spell-checkers were added, they enabled a new generation of writers to write notes, letters, messages, books, and documents of just about any kind. The integration of word processing into computers has resulted in perhaps 2 billion users of word processing systems, including WordPerfect, Google Docs, and other open source applications; more than an estimated half billion people use the most popular program, namely Microsoft Word.

Word processing is intelligence-aiding software that has had a tremendous impact on our society. Only sixty years ago, one could distinguish between the educated and uneducated by their ability to write a letter or a note. If they couldn't spell or could not use correct grammar, their shortcomings were obvious. Spell-checkers, thesaurus options, and grammar checking are raising the bar. Of course, spell-checkers are not always accurate. They sometimes provide false confidence, so there still needs to be a mind behind the machine. Only context can provide the proper choice between words like *council* and *counsel.* Nevertheless, word processing has enabled people to write comments, letters—even books—when they otherwise would not have. This improvement in the ease and quality of written communication has contributed substantially to culture and science. While the computer was the key achievement of information technology in the twentieth century, word processing brought the most benefits to the population at large in the first decades of computing.

Speech recognition (SR) technology that converts speech to text has become increasingly reliable and is beginning to enter mainstream use, with the expectation that most people will routinely use it by 2020. Specialty applications include a speech recognition service that transcribes telephone messages into email or text messages, so that a person need not answer the telephone or listen to messages during meetings, conferences, or cultural performances, for example. An important benefit of such services is that they inherently provide documentation of the message: the receiver need not take notes, as listening to a voice message sometimes requires.

These systems are also integrating elements of natural language understanding, and their grammar support is improving. Predictive text systems are also increasing. Such software remembers a person's most-used words and makes suggestions when the first characters are typed. Some users may consider such systems a nuisance if they frequently predict the wrong word, but those using specialized language—for example, a surgeon who frequently uses such terms as *salpingo-oophorectomy* or *Nissan fundoplication*—may welcome them.

Worldwide, communication preferences are shifting from voice to text. While the telephone was the preferred way to communicate during most of the twentieth century, data transmission, including texting and email, is rapidly replacing voice in the twenty-first. A study by Ericsson showed that in December 2009, total mobile data traffic (mainly text, but also internet browsing, GPS, and other apps) surpassed voice traffic.[51] Worldwide, young people prefer texting over telephone calls and even email. Parents often cannot reach their children by telephone (even by smartphone). Even an email may or may not generate a response over the course of a week, but a text message usually stimulates a quick one. This phenomenon is increasingly applicable among people of all ages, particularly as parents and grandparents learn how to use texting to stay in touch with family.

Except for smartphones, mobile phones generally use the numeric keyboard for character input, requiring up to three or four clicks until the appropriate character is entered. As a result, such communications stimulated a new form of language usage. Single letters replace words where possible: the word "ate" becomes 8; "for" becomes 4; "to," "too," and "two" become 2.[52] Two other important factors are driving this movement: (1) each text message is limited to 160 characters (including spaces), and (2) some wireless carriers charge individually for text messages. So, textual shortcuts allow senders to communicate more information at lower cost in a single text message than "proper English" forms that would require multiple messages. In response to these factors, and without standards or government regulations, a type of digital text shorthand has developed that is growing in international use. Some believe this textual "shorthand" is a fad that will fade as more smartphones with QWERTY keyboards are adopted. Others believe that these short-

---

51   "Mobile Data Surpasses Voice," Ericsson Press Release, March 23, 2010. http://www.ericsson.com/thecompany/press/releases/2010/03/1396928.

52   For details, see http://en.wikipedia.org/wiki/SMS_language or http://www.webopedia.com/quick.../textmessageabbreviations.asp or www.netlingo.com/acronyms.php.

cuts will simply continue to evolve, even on the full keyboards that smartphones offer.

In the next decade, it is expected that the market will accept virtual keyboards. These are keyboards projected on any flat surface, such as a table or wall, and are larger than a small mobile device can offer. Combined with speech recognition, other sensory input devices, such as more sophisticated hand and finger movements or special glasses or lenses, could make the data input process more intuitive and easier.

There is also a trend toward simplifying and streamlining our language communication processes. Email may not always formally "greet" the person to whom the message is sent: "Dear…" may not be inserted above the message itself. Certainly, it is the exception for text messages to include such a salutation. Thus, electronic communication practices demonstrate that text and email communications are less formal, shorter, and more to the point, using shortcuts for convenience and adopting a different structure than that used in traditional written communications. They require focusing on concise communication that encompasses the essence of the intended message. Think for a moment about going to your doctor. Assume that you will have an exchange of questions and answers and go through a description of your health-related experiences. Many unforeseen emotional issues may guide the conversation. You may not get to the core issue until the end of the encounter. Now consider formulating an advance email containing a concise description of your medical history, reasons why you want to see the doctor, what the doctor should know about your condition, your past experiences, and so on. Such advance communication lays the groundwork for a more complete, effective, and efficient face-to-face meeting.

Our mind processing needs to change from the traditional storytelling mode to a logical, precisely formulated, focused mode that organizes data to cover the full context of the information to be communicated. Similarly, future bank requests, job applications, contract negotiations, corporate decisions, and much more will depend on skills for presenting a logical, precise, structured, and well-developed case. Professional interactions in sales and related professions that use "socializing meetings" to exchange information will have to recognize that the customer often doesn't have time (or patience) for sales talk that poses as socializing. I predict that sales approaches must change in their presentation style to be precise and brief. Of course, they also have to change in their overall prospect identification approaches and lead follow-up. Social media, internet research, and identifying appropriate prospect groups are professional techniques that did not exist twenty years ago; their full potential and impact are yet to be experienced.

From Data to Knowledge

The terms *information* and *knowledge* are not clearly defined or differentiated by the general population and are often used interchangeably (even in this book). Simply put, knowledge is *validated* information. "Validated" does not always mean "correct." Consider science as an example of validated knowledge. Science, research centers, and universities pose theories and subject them to the test of falsifiability, i.e., they seek to validate them by demonstrating (beyond reasonable doubt) that they are unfalsifiable. Sometimes, individuals unaffiliated with mainstream research and educational organizations create new theories. These, too, need to be discussed and tested. Each piece of knowledge, every belief system or theory, should be given the test of falsifiability. Information should be identified as lacking confirmation unless clearly proven to be correct or incorrect, but it should still be considered.

The history of alchemy, which spanned at least 2,500 years, demonstrates the difference between questionable research information and validated knowledge. Alchemists experimented with substances—particularly fire, metals, and chemical interactions. Usually sponsored by a ruler who hoped that gold could be produced by tinkering with metals, alchemists' explorations led to real knowledge that evolved into our natural sciences.[53] Most of their results were proprietary, and many of their experiments were done

---

53   Hans-Werner Schütt, *Auf der Suche nach dem Stein der Weisen: Die Geschichte der Alchemie.* (Germany: C H Beck, 2000).

to demonstrate principles of contemporary belief systems. They produced information, and when universities studied, debated, and tested these processes, the portion of it they agreed on became knowledge.

Knowledge within Belief Systems

Thought leaders through the millennia have wondered, "What is real?" The Greek philosopher Plato raised this question in the famous cave allegory, where fire and shadows create a different sense of what is going on than direct observation would.[54] Since then, thinkers of all fields have pondered what is real when the context is different from what it is believed to be.

Images and their interpretations are one thing, but the most important conversion of data into meaningful context is done by making sense of the data points in life. Connecting them—some real, some assumed, some part of a knowledge system—creates context. It can be argued that context assembly or belief system creation is the most critical step of all information processes. The various bits of information are assembled to fit into a belief system. In this process, some information that does not fit is rejected; other information is made to fit or is given priority according to its influence on other meaning within the belief system. For example, take statistics, which have the objective of arranging data in the form of numbers to make a point. Darrell Huff states, "The secret language of statistics, so appealing in a fact-minded culture, is employed to sensationalize, inflate, confuse, and oversimplify."[55] I would even go one step further and suggest that statistics are often used to prove a point and not to represent a factual status. Likewise, numbers as data elements can be arranged in many ways. And, the way a ques-

---

54   For a demonstration of the cave allegory, see this flash animation by the British Museum at http://www.ancientgreece.co.uk/knowledge/story/sto_set.html.

55   Darrell Huff, *How To Lie With Statistics* (New York: W W Norton & Company, Kindle Edition, 1993), location 10.

tion is formulated can, and may indeed be intended to, stimulate a desired response or conclusion.

Here we must drill deeper into belief systems. Most people are aware of their religious and political belief systems, but these obvious ones are just the tip of the iceberg. Each of us has hundreds of belief systems that govern daily information processes and influence our thinking, our decision making, our opinions, our preferences, and our prejudices. Belief systems mediate our personal environments and the professional, political, and scientific concepts we have acquired. Personal belief systems include concepts we carry with us about our health, our educational progress, our appearance, our ability to earn more money, and other internal opinions about our capabilities. Socially, we have belief systems about the people around us, the way personal relationships should be conducted, our neighbors and neighborhoods, our employer, the organizations with which we interact, and our friends and the way they live, just to mention a few. As for the wider world, we have belief systems about conflicts in our society, education systems, damage to the environment, health epidemics, the strength of a nation, international politics, and climate or nuclear issues, again to cite just a few.

Most belief systems are not directly expressed. They are anchored within us and govern thinking processes, as well as decisions, without our explicit awareness. Intelligence requires questioning our practices of converting data into information. Data elements are the building blocks of information; the way such elements are arranged may or may not represent the "truth." It is worthwhile to understand that the bigger issue is how we fit information and knowledge into the various belief systems we each carry with us as the source and guidance for our information processing and decision making.

At the data and information processing level, two types of distortion may occur. In one type, data may be sensed incorrectly or may be interpreted according to inappropriate rules or faulty assumptions. The second type is the brain's purposeful distortion of information: using data for a deceptive or untruthful statement—we might call it a lie. There are several types of deception, including perjury, bluffing, barefaced lies, contextual lies, withholding information, emergency lies, exaggerations, fabrications, jocose lies expressed through teasing, sarcasm, even storytelling; lies by obsolete signage, obsolete or false identity, and false or inadequate information about a product. There are also so-called lesser lies: puffery (advertising exaggerations), noble lies (often told to maintain law, order, and safety, or not to offend someone), and lies to protect the innocence of children.

Lies are the smaller part of incorrect information distribution. The larger part consists of data that are heavily tainted or misrepresented through the belief system of the person generating them. There is individual interpretation and bending of fact according to belief systems. And there are governmental, corporate, and organizational information spinning, image distortions, reputation management, and public relation campaigns in which the goal of correct information is given up for other purposes. Think of people who promote information that seems very unlikely and far-fetched (or even clearly false) to you, but they believe it. Their community may be based on a belief system that validates that information as "knowledge." In other words, they and their similar-minded friends (in the online sense) believe in the information that seems incorrect to a person who does not subscribe to the same belief system.

So, what is truth? Each person has to decide. Taking into account all these information-processing complications, one must ask: Aren't we exposed daily to some kind of lie; that is, some kind of distorted information processing? Is there anyone who does not lie at some time or another? Or is reality just a very complex perception? What is truth, and what do we mean when information is in accord with fact or reality? To a great extent, each person has to decide what is believable and what is not. The challenge of the new information society, where many outrageous opinions, prejudices, baseless theories, and even conspiracies circulate, requires that one use available validated information to navigate toward truth. The balance between naively believing information and determining the basis of information and rejecting what we find invalid will be very important in the future.

During information acquisition, the brain decides whether information fits into a current belief system or if a modified or new belief system is warranted. At an early age, beliefs are formed by acquiring information from parents, peers, teachers, and nowadays, public media—particularly television and computer games. All information acquisition is indexed and sorted according to the belief systems a person has adopted (until they change). This explains why people who belong to different political parties can interpret the same information very differently. If you read about the same news event in multiple newspapers, you may find that each presents a very different interpretation of the same event. When a politician is a candidate for office, the path to success is not through a true description of post-election intentions, but through appeal to popular belief systems with information that fits them. But belief systems that interpret data and information differently are not limited to political ones. On the national level, belief systems govern the cultural and economic agendas of a nation. For example, in the US, wealth creation is a key ingredient of the national belief system, while in Western Europe, social justice dominates. Looking at past and current conflicts, one can conclude that belief systems cause wars. No other single element has killed as many people as clashes between belief systems. They govern much of religious belief, behavior, which opinions we hold, what we think of our neighbors, what we believe of strangers who may act or look different, what we dare to do, how we interpret others' actions, how we judge employers and colleagues…in short, what we think is right and what is wrong, what we believe we can get away with, and what makes us compliant. Our knowledge is dependent on our belief systems, as are our actions.

In the past, political belief systems were promoted and defended by nation-states. This has changed with WIC. A belief system may have followers from completely different countries and backgrounds. Future information management will have to try to manage belief systems. Whereas conflicts over belief systems used to lead at times to war, today, some people try to attract attention to a belief system through terrorist acts. An opportunity exists through WIC to wrestle in words rather than use violence. The challenge is the creation of methods that allow the peaceful interaction of belief systems, ideas, or convictions. This involves analyzing information and ensuring that it is believable (validated).

From Knowledge to Wisdom

So far, we have followed how data are interpreted as information and how information is validated to become knowledge. But what about wisdom? One interpretation is that wisdom causes people "to choose or act or inspire to consistently produce the optimum results with a minimum of time, energy or thought."[56] Robert J. Sternberg describes different approaches to wisdom, namely the philosophical, implicit-theoretical, and the explicit-theoretical approaches.[57] But there is no sufficient distinction between what is smart or clever and what is wise. I am inclined to follow the European understanding of wisdom, which is based on a sufficient amount of knowledge and intuition in order to aspire to act, speak and think. In other words, wise decision making does not bring money, power, acclaim or other worldly goods. It focuses on fairness, sustainability, ecological concern, and ethical-moralistic beliefs; it covers the tensions between knowledge and intuition and requires maturity, consideration for others' feelings and needs, and a distancing of oneself from competitive survival/success factors. Similar to happiness, which is not a condition but is achieved only transiently, wisdom can only be experienced during limited times of heightened recognition. It is something people should strive for, similar to Buddha's goal to achieve the ninth level of awareness. Wisdom is far more than smartness. One becomes rich or powerful or socially successful by being smart. Coming up with solutions when challenged involves smartness. In contrast, being wise is not about any of these competitive motivators. Wisdom values universal fairness and considerations beyond individual gain. Wisdom concerns the general good. Wisdom is not selfish. It is living for a good cause.

Some studying the meaning of wisdom have linked it to aging and say it is found most often in older people. One might say that

---

56 "The World's Wisdom on Your Side" (quoting Wikipedia on Wisdom), Sources of Insight, July 7 2011. http://sourcesofinsight.com/the-worlds-wisdom-on-your-side/.

57 Robert J Sternberg, *Wisdom, Intelligence, and Creativity Synthesized* (Cambridge, UK: Cambridge University Press, 2003), 147–151.

is no surprise. At an advanced age, the decline of life motivators mean decreased ambition (for instance, less interest in earning big bucks) and lower sex drive. This combination might enable people to have more emotional resiliency, since emotions and human drives may be less than those of a younger person. Experience and disappointments might enable a wise person to be more open to other beliefs and possibilities. And the ability to look at one's own mistakes, rather than blaming others for their consequences, might be mixed with forgiveness and humility. But it would be wrong to assume that wisdom comes automatically from old age or that it can only be achieved in old age; one should strive to achieve it much earlier. Wisdom is the highest level of coordinating one's belief systems.

Information Overload

Besides making sense of information and distinguishing between correct and incorrect information within the context of our belief systems, we are challenged to manage the flood of information that is addressed or accessible to us. As already noted, people have long complained that there is too much information to manage. The internet has intensified this feeling, and it will only increase. We are flooded with general information from radio, TV news, newspapers, and blogs, with person-directed information (mail, junk mail, email, text messages, phone calls, and so on). Years ago, I used to read one or two newspapers, plus a few magazines, regularly. Today, I check out various sections of six to ten enewspapers, some of them from different countries. As a typical symptom of this wider information access, information acquisition is done according to topic and geographical interest. I am not reading more, but I am reading with more of a focus. The key to focused information is indexing, whether done by the reader or by a service such as Google News. In general, indexing will assist with future information use and determine what kind of information is sought. Current algorithms for accessing information are somewhat dangerous, since they first bring up the information most used or last accessed. When the last accessed or most used information is presented first in a web search, it is easy for a person to find no challenges to a present belief system. Industries, politicians, and others must stimulate or influence people to look at new things or from new perspectives. Surely, over time, other ways of creating priority displays will become available.

The Meaning behind Information and Knowledge

When you read a book, watch a movie, or observe a theater play, you are taken in by the story. If it is a good or fascinating story, its events and descriptions capture your imagination. The way events are presented to your perceptional inner image creates feelings. The virtual experience of situations may provide stimuli and insights. In the information society, the goal must be to understand the deeper meaning of a story. We must look beyond what people do and say. For instance, a movie may portray a cleaning woman entangled with a man outside the family who stimulates her to read a book and enter the world of thinking games like chess. If well depicted, one can become fascinated by the actress and actor and how they deal with emotions and admire their surroundings. Even more, the moviegoer should ask, what is the message the producer wanted to give? In this case, the message might be that any person can be empowered by reaching out to different information systems and find new meaning.

We are just at the beginning of semantic software that, within seconds, can extract relevant subject matter information out of thousands or millions of pages. Topics, papers, and books will be processed according to their open and/or underlying messages. This mining of concepts and ideas will become a new information management industry. There is a need for summaries and main messages to be attached to any book, movie, theater play, and so on. This need is the result, not just of information overload, but also of the opportunity that WIC offers to enhance our knowledge capital. Managing the unimaginable wealth of information forces us to mine its core and gain the most from it.

How to deal with too much information and how to find desired data within its huge pool are challenges of the future. Information technology will have a major role in influencing people as politics, parties, corporations, and other organizations develop sophisticated methods to advance their belief systems. Debates over net neutrality are just one aspect. As informatics professionals and politicians debate how WIC can provide fair and open information in the future, interests and belief systems will inevitably clash.

Compare the information industry to the financial industry. Both provide critical currencies that keep modern societies going. Just as there are regulations for banking, regulations are needed to guarantee key information principles such as free access to information, transparency, independent fact-checking, and information management systems that assure the timeliness and essential responsiveness that will best advance our knowledge capital.

6

The Virtual World

As noted earlier, the ability to struggle with the concept of death and to capture abstract concepts of supernatural forces and other belief systems is a key distinction between the human intelligence system and that of animals. Our early ancestors developed imagination skills that go beyond providing for daily life: the search for food, the struggle for survival and protection against others, and ways to reproduce. The ability to form mental images, sensations, and concepts when they are not part of directly sensed reality opened up a whole new world of concepts, visions, and ideologies. This was the beginning of the virtual world, a phenomenon that has become more complex over time, but only now has reached the tipping point where it will transform and characterize our times.

It is difficult to find a good definition for "virtual." People use it in connection with many computing and communication activities. Virtual computing, virtual businesses, virtual medical treatment, virtual education, virtual offices, virtual art, virtual sex, virtual particles, virtual philosophy, and virtual relationships are just a few examples. For the purpose of this discussion, let's assume that "virtual" means that some person, object, concept, process, or image is invented, or it is replaced or complemented with something that performs the same purpose or function as the (real) original. For instance, instead of actually being with a friend at the same physical location, an exchange of transmitted electronic images creates a "virtual" meeting across distances. Or, instead of going into a shop and talking to a salesperson, the online store "virtually" provides all the information you need to select a product while you are at home (or wherever you are with your mobile device). But the seemingly unreal world of virtuality goes even further.

There are three types of virtual applications. In the first, fantasy and imagination replace real-life scenarios. Imagination and creativity are commonly considered good information processing features, as they are a necessary ingredient to the universal move toward greater complexity and information system improvement. But then, we also have delusion, with its negative reputation. Everyone has belief systems, but delusion makes a person hold onto and vehemently defend a belief that others recognize as mistaken or impossible to substantiate. In other words, delusion is a belief that does not appear acceptable or real to others.

The second type of virtual application concerns research, discoveries, scientific knowledge, and belief systems that cannot be verified easily with our bare senses. These can only be understood with the help of belief systems or technical devices. Think of the micro world of bacteria, microbes, or viruses, which we cannot see without microscopes. They are not part of the world of "real" human sensations, where we are limited to our own sense capabilities without technical support. Think also of a large magnification that opens a world of actively moving molecules in place of the solid surface we see with the naked eye. One must believe in the technical devices that open such worlds to us. We accept these worlds as real, even if we need mechanical assistance in the form of magnification to sense them.

The third virtual application is the substitution of people and their activities with technology. This movement started in communication. First, one spoke to a telephone set connected with a wire rather than to a person. Then, one listened to the sounds coming out of a box called a radio that provided the speech and music of people who were not present. The addition of images with TV increased virtuality as people who were not really there visited us in our living rooms. Wireless communication heightened this experience: people felt they were speaking into a device that sent their words through the air. "If we could only see the messages that swirl around us in the air" expressed how some people wondered about this virtual miracle. The difficult process of adjusting to virtuality is shown when journalists and others ask, "Would you trust your cell phone concerning your health?" It implies the question, "How can this little (stupid) device give me advice on health matters?" But the device is just a part of WIC, a connected web with a thousand times the knowledge content of your local doctor.

People of the past listened to stories of imaginary events, and many listeners may have embellished or distorted the story in their own minds. Storytelling used to be a community event for people of all ages, an opportunity to listen and to use their imaginative skills. Eventually, religious rituals, music, poetry, debates, and other events offered people opportunities to think or experience life outside daily chores. The process increased in refinement as actors added improvisation. In the Greek tradition, three types of drama (tragedy, comedy, and satyr), introduced virtual life into the thinking process. In the Egyptian and other African traditions, theaters stimulated thoughts of the gods. In India, hundreds of plays were written until the tenth century, but after the Islamic conquest, theatre was discouraged or forbidden.[58] In the Chinese tradition, music, drama, and acrobatic displays included virtual actors such as puppets.

Only a small percentage of the population—the privileged— were historically exposed to the virtual experiences of theater and books. Books opened up a window into other people's lives: personal relationships, life's ups and downs, happiness and misery, and unfamiliar customs and cultures could all be experienced. Fiction describes, in part or whole, invented and/or imagined events. Reading fiction, whether in poetry or narrative, allows the reader transcendence into a virtual life. This has been helpful, if not a cure,

---

58   Wikipedia: http://en.wikipedia.org/wiki/History_of_theater.

for many people trapped in boring or depressing situations. A good novel can be the "information drug" that can lift the spirit and let one forget about present circumstances. Other books can provide the feeling that one's misery is not unique. Whether uplifting, depressing, or just generally informative, books have had a tremendous impact on people's lives. Their sheer volume is enormous. Google has identified 129 million books for its scanning project, in which it intends to make many or all of these books digitally available.[59] Books have provided more virtual life to people on this planet than anything else. Now, they themselves are becoming virtual through ebooks, computer-based virtual versions of information storage and processing for book-styled text and images.

The virtual world not only applies attributes and scenarios to written fiction, but it also offers the opportunity to listen to someone "through the wire." As with much of technology development, this started with "one to many" transmission. The radio could send voice or music from one sender to millions—allowing politicians, for example, to spread their belief systems (good or bad) to millions of people. For instance, the Nazis would probably not have had so great an impact without being able to reach millions of people via radio. At the same time, the radio enabled positive virtual experiences, such as sitting in a dark family room and listening to a radio story, each person creating an imaginary world from sounds and words heard far from their originating source.

The technologies of sound transmissions were a wonder, changing societies and spreading information in unprecedented ways. When image was added through television, people lost some of the imaginary scenes they created when listening to radio. The twentieth century also saw the virtualization of theater performances through movies. Unlike live performances, movies enabled the same scenes to be seen in hundreds or thousands of places. Then the same pattern seen in many other technologies emerged: what was once under centralized control became available to everyone:

---

59 Joab Jackson, "Google: 129 Million Different Books Have Been Published," *PC World,* August 6, 2010. http://www.pcworld.com/article/202803/google_129_million_different_books_have_been_published.html.

instead of having to go to a movie theater, one could view movies at home.

Now, the internet is replacing real experiences with virtual representations and is opening virtual paths not imaginable before. This new world of virtual relations, virtual interactions, virtual communications, virtual procedures, and virtual games is changing our societies dramatically. A trip from one continent to another that might have taken weeks or months until a hundred years ago now takes about a day by plane. But now, in only seconds, one can make a virtual visit around the globe and connect with anyone just about anywhere at any time.

But it is not just the speed of virtually connecting with others that is changing our lives. Right now, the complete impact of virtual experiences can only be imagined. Over the last two thousand years, leading scholars have emphasized that it is not so much the task of absorbing new information from books that changed scientific study, but rather the exchange of arguments, the proposal of ideas, and their rejection that stimulated information processing in minds. In other words, exchanges and debates enable inventive thinking and stimulate people to consider alternative solutions. In the past, such communications were limited to a few people in a room within a specific university or other place of scientific or intellectual discourse. Now, debates and other discussions can be held worldwide, increasing participation possibly a hundred- or thousandfold. English as a *lingua franca* helps, but so do developments in new, intuitive language translation software.

Global Virtual Community

The internet and new smartphones have created a global virtual community that is having a major impact in many areas. It enables digital business, digital population control, and digital communities. The latter may have the most obvious impact on the way people communicate and form their belief systems. For hundreds of years, it was the village or city neighborhood that determined people's friends, associations with neighbors, and personal interactions. Now, relationships are created through virtual networks that link strangers who have similar personal or professional interests. People can be social while sitting in front of their desktop computer or while walking, waiting, traveling, exercising, listening to music, attending a meeting, playing golf, hiking in the woods, or gardening, just to mention a few activities where a mobile device can be used to connect with others. Thus, the very fabric of communities is changing.

At the first level, there are the large, commercial communities of acquaintances who take pride in adding more and more people as "friends" to tell what is going on in their lives. Others hope this kind virtual interaction results in job offers or personal introductions. They are not friends in the traditional sense, but are only loosely connected, with the potential to become more acquainted. Many people move on to create a more intimate community where it is safe to report more sensitive personal experiences. This second level of internet community will replicate the traditional family in some of its features, particularly trust, a common inclination to help each other, and a feeling of ease with one another. A third level of wide-ranging communities is also being developed according to hobbies or interests. These communities expect support in return for interesting information, public relations, and other contributions to the cause of the specific community's belief system. For instance, if you are interested in a particular style of music, you will be informed when there are new recordings or performances and of subject-related news. In return, you may support the community with financial or informational resources, such as experiences or opinions that you share. In the years to come, our society will be transformed into a wide range of virtual communities, some covering the globe, others remaining localized. These communities will play a major role in the competition between belief systems, since ideas will be carried out into virtual circles. Rather than in letters to a congressman or local newspaper, opinions will be expressed and processed in virtual communities.

Virtual Wars

But there is a dark side. WIC also brings virtual weaponry. Human warfare used to be focused on developing physical weapons that kept the attacker out of enemy reach. The ideal weapon attacked from thousands of miles away. Now, we have developed robot-like, unmanned aerial vehicles (UAVs): aircraft remotely controlled by artificial intelligence that may include sensors, weapons, or other purpose-driven equipment. In 2011, there were reportedly fifteen thousand virtual warriors available for ground deployment, seven thousand for the air, and an undisclosed number in the sea.[60] When equipped for flying, they can take off, land, and fly by themselves, using artificial intelligence. Operators can program a destination and concentrate on mission logistics and decision making while the UAV takes care of everything else. For the operator, the work may seem like an extension of digital games. To understand the importance of virtual war, consider that the US Air Force reportedly trains more UAV operators than it does traditional pilots.

Of course, these developments are not limited to the United States. More than forty countries are said to be experimenting with such robots.[61] Will this be a bigger threat to the survival of this planet than the threat of nuclear weapons? One can imagine that terrorists and enemies might try to bring parts of such virtual weapons into a country and then remotely send a swarm of them to a destination. Virtual war ultimately dehumanizes violent conflicts. War is performed without the drawbacks of counter-attack and collateral damage. It is both psychologically and physically easier to press a button to launch a missile that will kill, say, five hundred people, than it is to stab them to death individually. Because the operator is absent from the action, an anesthetic situation is created, and accountability for outcomes falls easily into the "just following orders, sir" mind-set. Also alarming is the concern that robotics will be used for civil functions such as controlling traffic, spying on people's movements, and so on. Some early examples can already be found in urban areas

---

60   Christian Caryl, "Predators and Robots at War," *The New York Review of Books,* Volume LVIII, Number 14, September 29, 2011.

61   Ibid.

and roadways. The potential of virtual control systems is often not taken seriously.

Virtual Industries and Virtual Personal Life

Banking is a forerunner in the field of virtual activities, with many other industries to follow. In healthcare, for example, a lone doctor will no longer have sole responsibility for a patient; through virtual collaboration, a team of clinicians will consider all aspects of a patient's life from birth to death, giving guidance in nutrition, exercise, medication, wellness, flexibility, selective surgery options, and more.

In business, a major transition is already well under development. The virtual office is a type of virtual community where a company's staff members work from their homes and across wide geographic distances. Contrary to early predictions, people can be more productive by focusing on work in private settings; in offices, colleagues can be a distraction and energy is diverted to office interaction. In rural areas, local newspapers are beginning to be replaced by digital communities that combine digital broadcasting with blogs for opinion exchanges and organize occasional virtual meetings.

New communication patterns are emerging in this virtual world. In the past, people wrote letters according to their needs to connect. A couple with an intense relationship might write each other daily letters. Others might send letters only when there was a need or expectation. The greeting card industry created customs to stimulate the sending of cards at birthdays, holidays, and significant personal events such as graduations, deaths, and illnesses. Separated families often had a fixed time, such as a Sunday afternoon or evening, to call and keep each other up to date on family matters, health, and activities.

Social networks are changing all this. Now, people routinely connect with others by tweeting, chatting, or exchanging other short messages. These messages are not just to report on special events. People often stay in touch even when there is nothing to report. Code words such as "meep beep" say "How are you? I care." In other words, a new generation increasingly communicates virtually, and their communications are not only for exchanging information, but also just to be in touch. As people participate in a number of virtual communities, they communicate a "personal status" to each. On Gmail or Facebook, for example, a person might post a status like "looking forward to Friday," "currently in a down mood," or "excited about a friend I met a few days ago." In business communities, messages such as "working on a new project" or "traveling to close a big deal" give others a sense of what is going on without giving particulars away.

Information acquisition that is not between colleagues or others with similar interests, or between teachers and students, should not be underestimated. Virtual education has had a slow start but has great potential. It may be decades before the hierarchical establishments of traditional schools, colleges, and universities transform into effective virtual systems of information transfer. The current classroom system is a batch-processing system, where a group of students is taught by one teacher. Virtual online teaching can be much more responsive to individual learning skills and needs because it is geographically unlimited and offers easier, more personalized learning opportunities with fewer distractions. The concern that students wouldn't learn through computers is similar to companies' concerns about productivity in virtual versus traditional offices. The curriculum of online education will have to change with the trend from passive listening to active interaction and participation. The combination of learning games and stimulation to explore knowledge subjects will turn education into a completely new information process. It will lead universities and colleges to change their business models as they adjust to creating online learning communities that will compete for students around the world.

Similarly, new virtual theater communities are emerging in response to difficulties in attracting customers to theaters. The audience watches at home at their convenience and according to their interest. For example, the Digital Concert Hall of the Berliner Philharmoniker, one of the world's top classical orchestras, offers live and recorded performances online. Some people find the virtual music experience superior to sitting in the bolted-down chairs of a concert hall. They can observe individual players and the conductor's style and emotions close-up. The Metropolitan Opera no longer needs to rely on the few thousand people who can attend a live performance; they are broadcasting to movie theaters globally, allowing thousands more to "join" the audience. On the negative side, such virtual art performances favor the well-financed and powerful institutions. The result will likely be a loss of theater diversity until smaller theaters recognize that they too can create their own virtual communities. A major advantage of virtual broadcasts is their ability to link to other virtual resources. For example, while listening to Mahler's 1st Symphony, a listener can research relevant historical and performance information on a smartphone or tablet. That is, virtual experiences are not just performances but include information that can enhance them.

Virtual systems also exist in healthcare. For instance, seniors can be monitored in case of a fall or other emergency. Virtual caregiver or clinician visits via TV, computers, and other devices allow the remote assessment of a patient's condition and the prescription of treatment. Some new homes have integrated electronic sensing devices that enable better monitoring and support. Virtual devices in the home are more reliable in measuring a patient's vital signs, such as blood pressure, than devices in the "artificial" setting of a doctor's office. There are also virtual systems for well-being. Digital systems provide virtual sounds such as soothing waves for falling asleep or chirping birds for waking. Such systems also guide and monitor individuals through exercise or recreational activities, such as bicycling or hiking.

The challenge of coping with an overwhelming information flow that no single individual can handle will increase. Many people already get hundreds of emails per day, much of it filtered into the spam folder—but filters sometimes misinterpret an important message as junk. News, blogs, and professional and personal information can overwhelm and may result in missed valuable information. One answer to this problem is specialized virtual networks where members exchange valuable information. This move toward a network of specialized information communities around each person has already begun and will expand.

We are just beginning to understand the impact of virtuality on our society. Location-based information gathering, marketing, and intelligence will become increasingly important factors. Where you are will become less important, because you will be able to access information from any place in the world. The future knowledge network will enable quick access to information and resources such as local news, and information about dangers, such as air quality and traffic jams. Car manufacturers are already including apps for detecting allergy levels on specific streets, for instance. Collective sensing provides researchers with information about group movement, the needs of subpopulations, and information flow. Virtual collective sensing will identify transportation needs, energy use, and more. Smart systems will identify data that allow planners and system providers to understand the needs of our society and how to most effectively and efficiently meet them. Of course, such systems could potentially be misused, so their development and implementation must be transparent and must address how to avoid, recognize, and address misuse.

The major challenge for this planet is to reach out into the universe (or multiverse) of billions of stars and yet-unimagined galaxy systems. The first generation of such exploration took us to the moon. In future space travel, we will aim to achieve what we have already accomplished on this planet. Just as virtual visits replace the exchange of ideas by people at real visits, so will space communication depend on creating an infrastructure for exploring regions that are far from present physical reach. Welcome to the new age of virtual life. The era has just begun. Working in virtual offices, having virtual friends, and conducting wars with virtual fighters mark only the beginning of a new virtual world.

7

Personal Impact:
From Literacy to Net Navigation

O ur current information system benefits from past information systems and developments. While a range of smaller steps have helped to make more and more information accessible to increasing numbers of people, what we are experiencing now is unprecedented, both in impact and importance. As noted, the six ingredients of a WIC are (1) computers, (2) computer software, (3) internet connectivity, including social media, (4) indexing of digitally available information, (5) mobile devices and apps, and (6) cloud computing. Together, they offer new communities, new knowledge acquisition and distribution, new forms of society, new paradigms for economics, and new research opportunities. These new opportunities will create new professions and jobs, while others will be impacted negatively or even lost. The slow move to more transparency and democracy can already be seen in political developments in North Africa, the Middle East, Russia, and elsewhere. But what about the impact on individuals?

WIC will affect everyone in five areas. The first is how information and knowledge are stored and accessed. Our society and all information functions are changing from being brain-centric to WIC-centric. Brain-centric meant that the brain was still the center of information storage and memory. A lawyer, physician, or scientist relied on memory, supported by books and other storage media according to need. As the volume of information grew, no individual could retain all the knowledge of any single field like law or medicine. WIC offers information that exceeds by a millionfold or more what the brain can store. Just think of the knowledge in several hundred million websites, well over 100 million digitized books (including all new books and documents created in digital form). As humans outsource their memory function to WIC, the brain is taking on a different function and is beginning to process information differently.

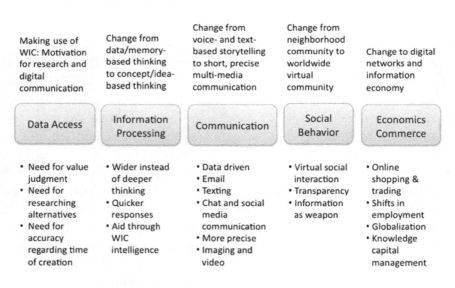

Figure 10. Changes WIC is bringing for individuals

Through WIC, people will experience some fundamental changes that will require a different method of accessing data and information. People who either opt not to take advantage of WIC or do not have the necessary financial means or infrastructure to do so will be disadvantaged. Perhaps a future political party will declare a person's right to access WIC. When the opportunity to be a citizen of WIC is available to anyone in any country, with any educational background and in any language, then people will have to be motivated to become part of WIC. This will require a very different attitude toward information. Knowledge acquisition methods will change from reading books, magazines, newspapers, and other media and listening to lectures, debates, and so on to online searches, streamed information, blogs, apps, etc. It will also include music and videos. This shift will be guided by an individual's curiosity, interests, belief systems, and other motivations. Knowledge acquisition will be furthered by indexing algorithms. Additionally, WIC will motivate people to research everything from restaurants to illnesses and from favorite musicians to available flights. Decision making will be guided by practical research that is facilitated by WIC.

The desire for information is a sign of our times, and people will demand that access to information not be limited by authorities. Because WIC is global, information will transcend national borders, and as translation systems improve, research and knowledge acquisition will no longer be limited by language barriers. Skills, information, and knowledge will be exchanged globally—scientific research results, disease management, videos on how to grow food or manage farm animals, and more. Instead of memorizing information, young people will be motivated by curiosity to acquire more information and skills to be successful in meaningful and satisfying careers.

The second area WIC will influence is the thinking process. In the human information processing field, a change from data and memory-based thinking to conceptual, idea-based thinking is already taking place. Belief systems are built on available knowledge; gaps are often addressed with presumptions. In the past, we tried to memorize ever more data to have them available when needed. WIC now provides an ever-expanding volume of data to facilitate the thinking process. While many new stimuli may discourage "deep" thinking, WIC will increase the "wide" thinking process that includes rapid data acquisition. (WIC will not eliminate deep thinking, which may be best facilitated when there are few distractions.)

The third area of change WIC will stimulate is in communication. Faster computer interactions require faster responses. Airplane pilots, today's drivers, and modern machine operators all need to make decisions and respond in split seconds. Information processing speed requirements were different a hundred years ago; decisions could be made over days or weeks. Digital games and other computer interactions now prepare people for fast information processing.

Long-winded voice communications (for example, telephone calls that start with "how are you" and proceed to a discussion of the weather before they get to the point), are changing to precise, short data communication that is to the point, occasionally supported by mood images. In general, communication is changing to involve more rapid and precise data and image (including video) exchanges.

The fourth area that WIC communication will change is social behavior. People used to center their lives around their families, neighbors, local acquaintances, people they met at social occasions, or people they used to know who were not nearby. WIC enables social interaction with anyone who is virtually connected, and distinctions will be made between those who choose to participate in WIC and those who do not.

In the millennia-old struggle for equality and democracy, a new level of transparency is available in WIC virtual society. Some see it as disruptive, while others desire or even expect it. This is part of the movement toward freer societies. Linked to more democratic behavior, transparency is the notion of freedom of information. People will demand increasing transparency from all organizations, including governments, corporations, and businesses. Organizations built on privacy (security authorities, government branches, secret services) may need to reassess what information can or should be made public and what can legitimately be excluded.

This move to transparency is one of the major societal changes WIC brings. The tension between old and new ideas about transparency was brought to the fore when WikiLeaks and others published sensitive information. In time, such disclosures will be both accepted and expected as people question why certain information should be kept hidden and whether keeping information secret is done to hide unacceptable behavior. But transparency is not one-sided: we should not demand transparency from large organizations if we are not willing to make our own personal lives more transparent. The loss of privacy and its effects will be discussed below.

Another of WIC's long-term social effects may be the use of information as a weapon. Current governments are working on "cyber war" weapons and have already successfully planted malware in enemy information systems and destroyed the central processing system of a military headquarters. Most cyber warfare will probably aim to destroy an infrastructure or information system to affect a country's economy. Governments have already placed viruses in adversaries' computer systems to cripple specific operations. Informational warfare can also stop an enemy force from attacking and keep a military system from defending itself. In fifty years, will most terrorist attacks and wars be replaced by informational warfare? Will informational violence be more acceptable than physical violence that kills people?

The fifth wave of change that WIC will bring is in businesses and jobs. Economics and commerce will continue to move from brick-and-mortar to online operations. This is a major change to the business environment, producing winners and losers. There is a parallel movement that gives the transition even greater impact. WIC enables many businesses to streamline operations by passing traditional employee functions on to the consumer (for example, orders self-keyed online rather than through a customer service representative). This leads to unemployment where people are no longer needed for traditional jobs such as in sales, travel, or banking. New information-based job opportunities will take some time to develop. Compare this to the disruptive introduction of the automobile.

When motors were put in carriages, tens of thousands of people lost jobs caring for and feeding horses. A whole industry collapsed. It was several decades before the motor industry grew strong and provided many more jobs than the industry it replaced. WIC's effects on some businesses and on job losses may be dire, but it is important to understand them in terms of information and knowledge capital. While old jobs will die, new opportunities will arise. One must try to understand such changes and use one's knowledge capital and WIC's rapid developments in order to survive.

Digital Hygiene

While people ponder whether the internet is changing people's thinking, we must remember that the internet is just one ingredient of WIC. Knowledge workers in today's society should be aware of their knowledge acquisitions and inventory of belief systems. All of us must also learn how to manage computers, navigate the WIC, and use available information to our advantage. We must learn how to communicate better with these technologies and understand that we can be held responsible for our communications years or decades later. We must recognize new opportunities in critical areas such as online banking or managing our own health information. Finally, we must learn and adhere to the do's and don'ts of "digital hygiene;" that is, how to function well with these technologies. Just as physical hygiene "refers to a set of practices perceived by a community to be associated with the preservation of health and healthy living,"[62] digital hygiene is a set of practices to follow in order to succeed within WIC. Such practices will help a person to make full use of the tools WIC offers and to identify strength and weaknesses according to one's knowledge capital.

Ideally, we should conduct knowledge autobiographies to identify what formed our intelligence and belief systems. Remember a teacher in Sunday school who influenced you? What did you learn from your parents, siblings, or school friends? This is a simple exer-

---

62   Wikipedia: http://en.wikipedia.org/wiki/Hygiene.

cise that helps us to understand, within limits, who we are and what our knowledge capital is.

Why is this important? On the one hand, identifying the forces that formed our intelligence and belief systems helps us to understand who we are, what we know, and why we like or dislike certain things. Sigmund Freud suggested that people should understand their behavior and then change it through rational insight. However, we can't be confident that rational insight and learned motivators will dominate in a conflict with basic life motivators. Nevertheless, an inventory of belief systems and an understanding of emotional motivators can be an important step toward establishing a deeper consciousness about the self.

Philosophers, neuroscientists, and others who study the mind and human information processing have long been curious about consciousness. At the base level, humans are aware of a self and of thinking, distinguishing us from animals, who are not believed to have self-awareness. However, it is not just self-awareness that brings the value of consciousness to the forefront, but also the awareness of one's knowledge, capabilities in information processing, and information acquisition history.

I am what I know. I distinguish myself from others according to my personal knowledge: what I know, what I believe, my prejudices, my interests, what I have read, what I suspect, and what I allege. Consciousness of all these information systems makes up a person's self-awareness in today's information society. Within someone's knowledge, belief, and information systems is another core intelligence system that defines a twenty-first-century person. This is our professional intelligence: the sum of our job or professional training and what we've learned in our careers. It defines our contribution to the world as well as our status within the society. The professional intelligence system includes both knowledge and skills. For example, a carpenter has learned how to work with wood and how to use specific tools to create or fix specific objects. The knowledge extends to materials and specific methods of working with them. A patent lawyer's professional knowledge capital may be in patents for plastic consumer containers as well as injection molding patents. The more unique fields of knowledge that we acquire that are responsive to the needs of society, the better our knowledge capital can be marketed.

Our personal information systems also influence our personal energy levels. We tend to procrastinate job functions that don't interest us, attending first to those that do. Knowledge capital requires that we understand these information processing influences. Personnel managers would do well to understand better what enhances or diminishes a person's inner energy. What influences our personal information processes influences the productivity of whole corporations and other organizations. If a company can create a climate of excitement, its employees will address their work with higher energy levels. This can be especially important in jobs that require creativity. Knowledge workers (and those in semi-knowledge worker positions) require mental energy to perform their jobs well. Performance declines when a worker is affected by an unexpected death, a divorce, a personal violation, a negative emotional motivator (such as humiliation), or a dislike of some aspects of the work. These examples are just the tip of the iceberg. Energy may be drained after a nasty argument at home, concern about a child, or anxiety about a relative or friend. Understanding the relationship between one's information system and emotions can help in addressing job performance.

A self-assessment of personal information systems and personal knowledge capital development requires a key ingredient: skill at navigating, taking advantage of, and managing one's interaction with WIC. This is digital hygiene, the set of practices that anyone who wants to function well within our information society should follow. Literacy was the bar for functioning as an educated person for millennia. If you couldn't read and write, your options were often limited to the low-paid, physical labor market. This labor market is being replaced by machines that will do much of the repetitive work, or at least will enable people to do the same work with less effort. However, one should not expect that physical work will not be required in the future. From cleaning services to furniture movers, manual work will still be necessary, but the number of people required for it will shrink. Whereas populations today are measured by literacy tests, in the future they will be measured according to their digital literacy and digital hygiene. By digital literacy, we mean "the ability to locate, organize, understand, evaluate, and analyze information using digital technology. It involves a working knowledge of current high technology, and an understanding of how it can be used."[63] Digital literacy is a step beyond computer literacy: it includes networking, cloud intelligence, knowledge about security, and knowledge management. It combines digital competence with management of WIC devices, software, threats, and opportunities.

Protecting Your Knowledge Capital

Digital competence requires the safeguarding of both one's information capital and data integrity and an understanding of one's particular privacy and security needs. Many people believe in a right to privacy. Politicians and the media often give the impression that not only do we have a strong right to privacy, but that we also can expect authorities to protect it. However, reality is different. The "U.S. Constitution contains no express right to privacy," states a website from the law school of the University of Missouri-Kansas City.[64] It continues,

The Bill of Rights, however, reflects the concern of James Madison and other framers for protecting specific aspects of privacy, such as the privacy of beliefs (1st Amendment), privacy of the home against demands that it be used to house soldiers (3rd Amendment), privacy of the person and possessions as against unreasonable searches (4th Amendment), and the 5th Amendment's privilege against self-incrimination, which provides protection for the privacy of personal information. In addition, the Ninth Amendment states that the "enumeration of certain rights" in the Bill of Rights "shall not be construed to deny or disparage other rights retained by the people." The meaning of the Ninth Amendment is elusive, but some persons (including Justice Goldberg in his Griswold concurrence)

---

63   Wikipedia: http://en.wikipedia.org/wiki/Digital_literacy.

64   "Exploring Constitutional Conflicts: The Right to Privacy, UMKC School of Law. http://law2.umkc.edu/faculty/projects/ftrials/conlaw/rightofprivacy.html.

have interpreted the Ninth Amendment as justification for broadly reading the Bill of Rights to protect privacy in ways not specifically provided in the first eight amendments. The question of whether the Constitution protects privacy in ways not expressly provided in the Bill of Rights is controversial. [65]

In other words, do not expect the government or others to automatically guarantee privacy. Government does collect personal data. To stop it would require convincing politicians to do so. Public cameras, trade and industry data collection, as well as other databases, profile everyone. If the trend persists, there will be even more collection in the future. Therefore, it is each individual's responsibility to create the privacy protection he or she wants. First, determine what you consider important to keep private. For example, I am not worried about someone breaking into my game apps or most of my other entertainment or daily living apps, nor do I specifically care about the privacy of my hotel or airline mileage programs. But I do care about my digital identity in financial matters. The FBI states,

"Identity theft involves the misuse of another individual's personal identifying information for fraudulent purposes. It is almost always committed to facilitate other crimes, such as credit card fraud, mortgage fraud, and check fraud. Personal identifying information, such as name, Social Security number, date of birth, and bank account number, is extremely valuable to an identity thief. With relatively little effort, an identity thief can use this information to take over existing credit accounts, create new accounts in the victim's name, or even evade law enforcement after the commission of a violent crime. Identity thieves also sell personal information online to the highest bidder, often resulting in the stolen information being used by a number of different perpetrators. Identity theft can be very difficult for consumers to deal with, as they often do not know they have been defrauded until they are denied credit or receive a call from a creditor seeking payment for a debt incurred in their name."[66]

---

65   Ibid.

66   FBI   2006   report.   http://www.fbi.gov/stats-services/publications/fcs_report2006.

Criminals steal identity by capturing account numbers and passwords (for instance, at ATM machines), by posing falsely as a bank authority and asking for identity information, by interfering with the internet traffic of email or other messages, by copying databases, by accessing or stealing postal mail, and by a variety of other means. Protection against this kind of crime starts with selecting passwords that are complex. These should include numbers, characters, and symbols (such as &,*, +, etc.). Also, it is important to have many passwords, rather than just a few. There are smartphone apps for managing passwords with extra security protection. In addition, the FBI recommends:

- *Never give personal information via telephone, mail or the Internet, unless you initiated the contact.*
- *Store personal information in a safe place.*
- *Shred credit card receipts and/or old statements before discarding in a garbage can. If you do not have a shredder, then use scissors.*
- *Protect PINs and passwords.*
- *Carry only the minimum amount of identifying information.*
- *Remove your name from mailing lists for pre-approved credit lines and telemarketers.*
- *Order and closely review biannual copies of your credit report from each national credit reporting agency (Equifax, Experian, and Trans Union).*
- *Request DMV to assign an alternate driver's license number if it currently features your Social Security account number.*
- *Ensure that your PIN numbers cannot be observed by anyone while utilizing an ATM or public telephone.*
- *Close all unused credit card or bank accounts.*
- *Contact your creditor or service provider if expected bills do not arrive.*
- *Check account statements carefully.*
- *Guard your mail from theft.* "[67]

There are many reasonably priced security programs that can protect your systems. Some security programs guarantee data integrity through encryption. Others create firewall protection for any computer. The desire to protect against consumer profiling or to correct one's

---

67   Ibid.

own consumer profiling is a question of personal belief systems. One person might consider consumer profiling a horror, while another might see some benefits in it. Some people insist on protected Wi-Fi services; others prefer convenience. Organizations or groups concerned about a secure communication environment should consider an encrypted virtual private network (VPN). For those concerned that websites they visit can be detected or who want to assure that others cannot capture their IP address easily, special security measures must be taken. For instance, using untraceable IP rotation will keep secret the websites the user has been visiting, allowing anonymous surfing and protecting privacy in internet operations.

Although governments and law enforcement agencies are working on stronger legislative measures to provide better cyber security, it must be stressed that WIC systems are too complex, and breaking into them is too tempting, for them to ever be fully secure. As noted earlier, banks have been robbed for hundreds of years and every time they plug security holes, criminals find another entry. The same is true with WIC.

Digital hygiene also includes taking responsibility for any transmitted or recorded information. Although some object to the principle of responsibility, and some European politicians are trying to create safeguards that let WIC "forget," WIC never truly forgets. Any recording or picture of unethical or inappropriate behavior, voice expression, documentation by email or on social media, or use of foul or explicit language has the potential to be accessed and used against its originator at any time. This fact should lead people to think first before emailing, texting, or saying something that could be damaging to them. This principle applies not just to personal communications and documentation, but also to corporate, government, and organizational notes, documents, and communications. Unless specially protected by specific software or laws, information will be discoverable.

Electronic Banking

Digital hygiene in the WIC era concerns the handling of computers, the internet, information, communication, and storage. Core industries and services, for example, online banking and the management of health information, must assure digital hygiene for their users. As noted, banking is now less about managing money than handling financial information transactions. Banks have made one of the more aggressive moves into WIC to take advantage of its benefits: lower costs, fewer personnel, higher client activity, and greater efficiency. Some banks have introduced systems with machines that can read checks and deposit them to specific accounts. Others allow clients to send scans of checks safely from home for deposit. Whether checks are scanned at ATMs or at home, or are replaced by online transfers, financial information processing is changing the way payments are being handled. As the paper check slowly disappears as a medium of payment, new transaction methods are arising. One is near field communication (NFC), where a mobile phone is tapped against a scanner for payment.

For the individual, online banking can liberate the money management process. Any transaction can be made from home on a desktop computer or on a smartphone while on the road. ATMs took about twenty years to reach 70 percent usage, so it will probably take some time until two-thirds of the population are using online banking.[68] Still, the general trend is similar to that of other industries: Let the customer be in charge online, reduce employee labor, automate processes for intuitive use, and expand services. Clearly, this is changing the banking industry. In years to come, a banking customer will be able to check car financing options online. Within seconds, one or more bank loans may be offered, including details of all costs and cash flow-adjusted payment projections. Mobile phone apps might guide customers in financial matters in much the same way a GPS system guides travelers. Investments, the direct buying and selling of shares, and similar functions will all be done through WIC.

Online banking is as safe as crossing the street: If you are not cautious, you can get hurt. Security will improve with time, but people will find a way to break into any system, even if rarely. Your comfort level with online banking depends on how you handle the

---

68   C Peter Waegemann and Claudia Tessier, *The Impact of mHealth* (Boston MA: mHealth Initiative, 2010).

key security issues. The quality of a password is critical. Banks use a variety of systems for them: some use password tokens that change every few seconds. Others use location services, planting a computer cookie that verifies that information is coming from you (or, at least, from your computer). Photo identification with automatic face recognition is not yet being used, but it will likely play a much greater role as systems become more refined.

For good online banking digital hygiene:

- Check your financial institution's website for their privacy policy and liability should you lose money through online banking. Understand if the bank will replace stolen money and how much.
- Understand the financial institution's safeguards for passwords, secure message transactions, location services, cookies, and automatic signoff after a certain period of activity.
- Request automatic text message notifications to alert you of transactions.
- Check your account frequently and be fully aware of the status of payments, transactions, cleared checks, etc.
- Use a complex password and change it periodically.
- Never leave a computer outside the home unattended when logged into a financial site.
- Keep location service on so that your banker knows the order is not from an unfamiliar site or remote location.
- Use caution in doing financial transactions over public Wi-Fi.
- Guard your identity. Do not respond to email or telephone requests asking for passwords, Social Security numbers, account numbers, or other critical information.
- Implement security improvements offered by your institution.
- Beware of viruses, spyware or "Trojans" that can record and transmit a user's keystrokes, giving thieves unauthorized access to computers and account information.

Cybercrimes are reportedly increasing, but it is unlikely that they will affect the average bank customer any more than physical bank robbery does. In online banking, managing your financial capital depends on managing identification as well as monetary and knowledge capital.

Your Health and Health Information

New WIC systems can potentially have both negative and positive effects on health. On the negative side, the computer use can itself be damaging. Sitting for hours in one position, whether it is in front of the TV or a computer, should be balanced with exercise and stretching. Contact stress, monotony, posture problems, and uncomfortable computer environments can be avoided with ergonomic workplace design. Lower back pain, neck pain, wrist and finger pain, and eye strain can be addressed with appropriate seating, chairs, and support cushions. Health risks within WIC are not limited to those of sitting in front of a computer. Studies of mobile phones' potential for causing cancer are inconclusive, as I discuss in Chapter 9.

Like banking, healthcare is information-intensive, but it is decades behind in responding to WIC opportunities. The quality of treatment a patient receives depends greatly on a doctor's access to relevant information, and the vast scientific body of medicine far exceeds what any clinician can memorize. Good treatment also depends on a physician's knowledge of a patient's medical history, including previous illnesses, prescribed and over-the-counter medications, family history, and many other factors, including all diagnoses and prescriptions by other physicians. Ideally, the doctor should not start with a blank page but rather should have access to as much health information about the patient as possible. However, much of the information a clinician actually gets depends on what the patient remembers to say at each short encounter and on that healthcare institution's own records of that patient. Patient information does not usually get transferred between healthcare sites.

Imagine intelligent beings from another planet visiting Earth, trying to make sense of our healthcare system. They would find that with modern technologies, humans have created good documentation for factories and power plants, buildings, and automobiles, but that almost no one has a complete, documented history from pre-natal care through the present. Most people leave health decisions to health professionals, with whom communication is limited to the occasional encounter. There is little use of digital communication in healthcare compared to that for online banking or with friends and relatives by email, text, and social media.

Doctors are beginning to realize that the body of medical knowl-edge has grown to a point where medical schools can no longer address it all. Information must be extended, updated, and enriched by newer and more complete information when practicing medi-cine. Nevertheless, they are slow to use WIC navigation systems or exchangeable electronic health record (EHR) systems. The vision of EHR systems that allow all clinicians in a hospital or provider organization to be fully informed about a patient is, after more than thirty years, only slowly being implemented. Such systems should allow doctors to see what clinicians in other provider organizations have thought, diagnosed, prescribed, or operated on, but EHR sys-tems to date generally fail to provide the interoperability that ena-bles such information access.

Further, doctors work within information silos. Exchanges are limited, partly because of data protection and privacy regulations. Patients can have key roles in a modern healthcare system based on WIC. First, they must determine the relative values to them of access to health information and of privacy. A deep-rooted fear of disclosure of health information has settled into our belief systems and culture. Perhaps it originates from times when illness was con-sidered a divine punishment, but it also stems from actual or feared misuse of health information by governments or employers. This perceived threat is promoted by the media and stories (many anec-dotal) of people losing their jobs or being otherwise hurt through a violation of their privacy. Everyone can evaluate the potential dam-age of losing the privacy of health information. Where one person might have a good reason to guard health information from others, another may not mind if, say, his or her high blood pressure condi-tion is known. The advantages of not fearing privacy violations are that more experts may be able to help, more treatment options may be available, and others may be able to fill in gaps the healthcare provider has not addressed. As with other sensitive information, security systems can help. Providers can be reminded to take extra steps to secure information. However, should you decide that the privacy of your health information does not outweigh the potential benefits of sharing it, you should let your healthcare provider know. Your clinic or hospital cannot neglect privacy regulations and laws, but they can find ways to encourage clinicians to legitimately share more of your health information with others who can help in the care process.

WIC requires that people be involved in many of its processes. Just as citizens of WIC check in remotely to book air travel, report events virtually, visit their bank virtually, and work from homes while fully involved in company processes, they should also participate in their healthcare. Indeed, such involvement is a significant part of managing the knowledge capital of the future.

Active participation starts with understanding and managing health information. In practical terms, this means that everyone should have a complete record of medical care and a copy of all related documents. In the United States, patients have a legal right to health information, even though providers may resist releasing it.[69] For obvious reasons, the information should ideally be in digital format. When I asked for my medical records in the 1980s, I received 88 pages of partially typed, partly handwritten data, much of it illegible. Scanning it into digital format did not help. No doctor is likely to read through so many pages of unorganized, difficult-to-read patient information.

What is needed is a concise data set about a patient that accommodates the needs of most, if not all, specialties. In the early years of the twenty-first century, the Continuity of Care Record (CCR) was created.[70] It is a standard dataset that includes insurance information, past and current diagnoses, therapies, medications, complaints, findings, social and family history, as well as addresses of former and other clinicians (in case there is a question about a diag-

---

69   HIPAA legislation. See details at http://www.hhs.gov/ocr/privacy/hipaa/ understanding/consumers/index.html.

70   *ASTM E2369 Standard Abstract: Continuity of Care Record* (West Conshohocken PA: ASTM International, 2005). http://www.astm.org/Standards/E2369.htm.

nosis or prescription): a snapshot of a patient's relevant past and current healthcare information. In other words, clinicians don't have to see a patient without any prior information. That would be like boarding a plane when the pilot and the on-board computer have no information about the plane or the weather conditions, for instance.

The CCR (also available as a Continuity of Care Document, or CCD, that works in healthcare legacy systems) can be printed out or put on a USB drive, even a mobile phone. A dataset like this can constitute a personal health record (PHR). Creating and managing a personal health record is one of the key requirements for being a responsible person in our time. It is a form of digital hygiene. One should also have PHRs for anyone in one's care, such as children and elderly friends and relatives.

Actively seeking information on WIC is another "must" for any WIC citizen. Very few people would buy a car from the first dealer they visit; most savvy buyers compare alternative models, features, prices, services, and so on. But in healthcare, most people assume that the doctor they see has all the knowledge necessary for good care. In fact, the doctor who may have the most relevant knowledge about your specific condition may not be in your part of town but rather halfway around the world. WIC makes it possible to communicate with a distant medical expert as well as with a doctor just a block away.

Most people with internet connections seek health information on the web. Research has shown that "of the 74 percent of adults who use the internet, 80 percent have looked online for information about any of fifteen health topics such as a specific disease or treatment."[71] It has been only ten years since the medical establishment warned the public not to trust the internet. Today, that warning is no longer valid. Certainly, incorrect information exists on the internet just as it exists in pharmaceutical ads or magazines, in books, or other sources. However, it is easy to find widely accepted information on the internet, because index-

---

71   Susannah Fox, *The Social Life of Health Information, 2011* (Pew Internet Research Center). http://www.pewinternet.org/Reports/2011/Social-Life-of-Health-Info/Summary-of-Findings.aspx.

ing systems are designed to display the most authoritative and sought-after information first. Thus, a person looking for health information is likely to be led to American Heart Association, Mayo Clinic, or other respected institutions relevant to the content area in which they are interested. Niche websites that may have unorthodox (and potentially misleading information) are more difficult to find.

WIC people seek health information not only from traditional, privileged, and recognized sources, but also from other patients. Increasingly, those with a severe condition such as a chronic disease, those born with a genetic defect chromosome, and those battling severe cancer are helping others in health information WIC communities by sharing what they have gone through, what helped and what didn't, and aspects of treatment or medication that their physician did not adequately prepare them for. Sharing helps people cope in daily life; virtual support groups are an increasing part of healthcare knowledge management. As younger people age and as privacy concerns fade, these communities will grow in size and influence.

This movement will go hand in hand with another underdeveloped field: communication in healthcare. In the distant past, doctors visited sick patients and communicated in depth. Today, the sick drag themselves into offices where doctors see them for perhaps ten or fifteen minutes each, all day long in a factory-like process. This may have worked well enough a hundred years ago, but not today, when communication, research, and treatment methods have changed dramatically. Many clinicians have not yet adopted today's better communication technologies. WIC makes it possible for patients to report symptoms and pain when they occur and to avoid treatments being prescribed without details of the patient's history. Both texting and email communication should be available 24/7. A patient shouldn't have to wait for an appointment to report pain. Even images of wounds or symptoms can be communicated at any time. This requires dramatic changes in healthcare delivery and workflow; physicians (and patients) may not quite be ready. As in other areas, WIC conditions, opportunities, and benefits will emerge only slowly in healthcare.

It is important to understand that new technologies will not disappear. WIC is changing our lives in many ways. Everyone will be affected, even those in remote areas. Therefore, we must meet the challenges that new information technologies will bring. Success, the potential improvement of living conditions, and the prospect of a better life depend on how we manage WIC. It impacts every facet of our lives.

8

Digital Companions, Not Robots, Will Change the World

Mobile phones have brought unanticipated communication advantages: routine or urgent communication can be made from any place at any time. This has created an unforeseen demand for mobile phones, which telephone carriers responded to by making enormous investments in wireless communication infrastructure. As a result, mobile communication has become the most widespread technological development of the early twenty-first century.

How did wireless telecommunications evolve? In 1965, Gordon E. Moore predicted that computer chip information processing power would double every two years as twice as many transistors were included on ever-smaller integrated circuit boards. This prediction became known as "Moore's Law." Amazingly, this trend has held for more than forty-five years and is expected to continue. Eventually, chips became small and inexpensive enough to use in portable devices. In other words, the wireless phone absorbed computing capabilities: they themselves became computers.

Add to this the software breakthrough for creating mobile phone apps. Apple Computer created programming rules that allowed easy, relatively inexpensive creation of software that combines information processing with memory (both within the device and through the internet). This allowed creation of the true "people's" computer because it allowed developers to create apps for anyone's daily use and guidance. The benefits may be financial, but more important, they help people with their daily lives. Soon, other companies introduced similar app development systems. There are close to a million apps, and more are introduced every day. Whereas most software has been written for business use, mobile apps reached out primarily to the individual consumer, from infant to business manager, from teenager to retiree. There are apps for just about every hobby, specialty, profession, or interest. Some are silly, some are serious; many are simple, and others are quite sophisticated. App development marks the beginning of an important new era in information technology: for most, computers can offer far more than just email and web surfing. Now, games, guides, and support and information resources have come to the forefront. Digital companions are becoming the supplementary intelligence that people use in many aspects of their lives. With their relatively easy development platform, apps could have a social effect similar to that of Gutenberg's printing innovation.

During the last ten years, other technologies have also been packed into mobile phones, among them the built-in camera. Their pixel quality is increasingly competitive with basic digital cameras. Every smartphone user can now take photographs or video and communicate a happy moment at a party or damage to a house, identify a part that needs replacing, document a dangerous pothole in the street, or illustrate a medical symptom for a doctor. These capabilities are changing the use of intelligence in communication systems.

As digital companions build on the other elements of WIC, they are having a greater impact on our lives than any other communication device. These small communication and computing devices far exceed the number of TV sets, cameras, or fax machines in use. Internet access through mobile phones exceeds that from desktop computers. Mobile apps entertain, inform, guide, support, and allow communication by voice, text, or image. In addition, they can collect information from sick, elderly, or health-conscious people to support the healthcare process. Indeed, the mobile phone of the future may act as a medical device that senses physical data and notifies a doctor automatically. Devices with motion sensors can call for help automatically if an elderly person falls. Some pedometers use sensors now to count a person's steps. These devices can also be set for "fencing applications" to monitor the locations of children, people with dementia, or even employees.

Mobile devices also provide personal or financial decision support. We can check out the menu, prices, and customer comments of a new restaurant. Digital companions enable virtual business decisions and transactions. Online banking, money transactions, stock trades, and many other activities can be done more quickly and efficiently. At a conference in 2009, a participant reported buying a house with his mobile phone. Someone else mentioned that he had purchased a $20,000 boat with his. No purchase or transaction seems too difficult or complex for the digital assistant.

These devices can find the information that professionals need, whether they are engineers who need formulas and building codes at their fingertips, or lawyers looking up case law and commentary. A physician can access diagnostic tools, and medical histories from the exam room. A real estate agent can collate school and community amenity information with the usual vital statistics of any property on the spot. Knowledge bases that in the past had to be memorized or looked up in books and other documents are now instantly available for application to the immediate circumstances.

In other words, the mobile device has become the essential digital companion. But many people say their phone screens are too small, the keys are inconvenient, and that touchscreen keyboards allow too many mistakes. In response, mobile devices are developing two form factors. There are convenient, small phones for quick communication, research, education, or game playing. Then, there is the larger tablet for extended activities, including editing, writing, accessing data, and better display of images. For reading books, showing a potential client an engineering drawing, or describing a medical condition to a patient with an anatomical image, the tablet or ebook format is more appropriate and functional than the smartphone. The dedicated ebook reader will likely become less popular, as will the dedicated navigation system. There is a clear trend toward digital companions that can offer a universal set of applications.

Managing knowledge capital is not just a matter of being computer literate. It is important for people to understand and use many of the functionalities that digital companions offer. This point warrants emphasis: The digital companion is not just a minimized computer with telephone capability, a camera, and wireless connectivity. It offers unique features: easier access to knowledge bases and adaptability for use in most activities. Location services offer security functions and other benefits. Below I will categorize and discuss the range of digital companion functionalities.

The Phone: Voice Communication

Voice communication was the original purpose of the mobile phone. The desire to make phones more user-friendly brought a wide range of additional functions, including voice commands, alerts, quick redialing, and more. The transmission of voice calls via the internet instead of through telecommunication carriers is having a major impact on the latter industry. Nevertheless, the trend is from voice communication to data communication. Short text messages are increasingly replacing long telephone calls and letters—even email itself.

When using a wireless phone, whether over the internet or through a telecommunications carrier, consider the following:

1. Do not let the phone distract you. Use the speaker function and voice commands when driving or when otherwise occupied.
2. Show respect for people around you: Do not speak loudly.

3. Protect your privacy: Do not voice confidential information, such as credit card numbers and your Social Security number. And again, do not speak loudly.
4. Use programs that convert incoming voice messages into a text message or email. This is useful for receiving messages when you are in meetings or otherwise unable to take calls or listen to messages.
5. Manage your contact list well by expanding and maintaining it as well as backing it up.

Data Communication

After word processing, email has most changed our society within the last fifty years. Email, the free, instantaneous delivery of communication, is widely used except where organizations still request original documents or facsimiles. Mobile devices allow receiving and sending email at any time from any place where connectivity exists. As a result, email no longer honors a clear distinction between periods of work and rest. Until a few years ago, it was acceptable to declare communication off-limits on holidays or other off-duty times. In the new era of knowledge working, this distinction is enforced less and less. A knowledge worker is often expected to be available to respond quickly to messages at any waking hour.

Because of the very low cost of sending large volumes of commercial email, any address is vulnerable to unsolicited messages (spam). While advertising on radio, television, or printed media is tolerated to a degree, identifying and deleting unwanted email messages is more annoying and feels abusive. Spam filtering still requires checking through spam mail to remain certain of not missing "good" messages. One response to unsolicited communication is to gather a virtual community, where communication is not interrupted with anything unwanted. In many ways, these are like "gated" information communities that do not admit outsiders. To participate, one must find "an open door" to that information community through an insider's recommendation or by befriending a community member.

Chat communication allows real-time online communication (by either text or voice) within a virtual community. As opposed to email, chat information is usually not stored and so cannot be retrieved. As our lives become increasingly dominated by virtual communities we create around personal and professional interests, chat communication will likely increase.

It should be noted that the small screens of mobile devices can require adjustment, and traditional mobile phone keypads require multiple keystrokes to enter alphabetical characters. While hundreds of millions of people have learned to be efficient with this kind of data entry, hundreds of millions of others reject it. Even at the high end of mobile devices, touchpad keyboards require skills and learning in order to be effectively used for professional documentation.

One great advantage of many of these systems is their language versatility. A writer can easily switch between two or more languages, including language-contextual spell-checkers and other support systems. Even whole sentences can be translated on the fly. Whole documents will be translated with increased accuracy as translation systems become more sophisticated.

Digital Camera

The competition in *seeing* between the digital camera and the human eye is in full swing. Above a 12-megapixel resolution, cameras capture information at about the same quality as the human eye. But digital images see less than we do. Eyes can move to take in a whole scene and can focus on specific areas; a competing camera would need an over 500-megapixel resolution to provide the same capabilities. The difference in camera sophistication is in pattern recognition and image analytics. For everyday applications, face recognition software is making progress, and government systems are using artificial intelligence to monitor and make sense of the information that thousands of cameras capture. In New York City alone, between two and three thousand cameras operate 24/7, requiring round-the-clock vigilance for suspicious activity. This is where automatic image analytics come into play. Besides security applications in government and other organizations, healthcare will increasingly use image analytics for X-rays and other clinical images.

Communication through pictures or videos is another exciting development. YouTube is a great example of its potential impact. One can use the smartphone's camera to record family events, to document an accident or criminal behavior, to send a picture of a rash or injury to a healthcare provider, etc. Additionally, new industries will serve the huge field of inter-language communication using videos and still images. Today's child, with a mobile phone camera, is prepared for the new world and its new roles for image capture and image transmission.

Browser

The internet is the strongest element of WIC. The combination of the smartphone or tablet and the internet, where one can instantly access an endless amount of valuable information, is very powerful. This is a relatively new professional or personal experience. Two factors influence the use of a browser: the first is a person's degree of curiosity. Some will ask, "Why would I bother to look something up?" Others will enthusiastically recognize WIC as a tremendous opportunity to expand their knowledge base.

The second factor is the ease with which information can be accessed. WIC surfing speed will increase. Smartphone connection speeds are increasingly important to consumers. Websites offer one-click purchasing, and search methods are being simplified. The goal of web browsing is easy and fast access. Individuals, societies, businesses, or governments that are more skilled in accessing information will be in a better position to advance and to compete. It will be a race among industries, telecommunications carriers, and internet companies to provide the necessary infrastructure.

Music

For thousands of years, the only way to access music was to play it or and listen to it live, in real time. It was limited to a "here and now" experience, except for the few who could remember and replay it by ear. The dream of recording and reproducing music came true at the end of the nineteenth century with the introduction of the phonograph. Thomas Edison, who patented it, intended it for recording and playing back telegraph messages. Music recording was an unintended consequence, but it changed the world of musical and sound information. It could now be accessed and enjoyed in virtual mode; that is, without attending an actual performance. For a hundred years, special media, such as vinyl records (of various speeds and sizes) and digital compact discs (CDs), required special devices for replay. All of this is changing with WIC. The smartphone replaces the record or CD player, adding storing and playing music to its already amazing range of capabilities. Today, a mobile phone or tablet device can store thousands of pieces of music and play them through high-quality earphones or loudspeakers. In years to come, external speakers, too, will become obsolete as the quality of smartphone speakers improves. Music has become digitally stored information, and a digital companion allows music listening at any place and any time.

Personal Digital Assistant (PDA)

By the late 1980s, certain computer functions were integrated with other computing and communication functions. The digital calculator became a low-cost commodity. A general memory function could manage the most basic of daily challenges: organizing a list of contact information for either personal or business use. Thus, the electronic address book was born. People no longer had to memorize contact information. Outsourcing it to a portable device for reference when needed became routine. Supporting human memory with note-taking functions, both keyboard-based and handwritten, was a natural step for the digital assistant. A digital calendar could be used to remind one of birthdays, appointments, and upcoming events. Over the years, these PDA functions, combined with the camera, email, better telephone functionalities, and data communication became more user-friendly, and all are now routinely expected as parts of the smartphone package. In 2011, a voice-based system allowing communication between an artificial companion and its user marked a significant expansion of the smartphone's role as a digital assistant.

Location-based and Geographic Information Management

Most smartphones have a chip that identifies, records, and transmits a user's location. This global positioning system (GPS) can be turned off for privacy if one is concerned about being tracked. However, if that's not a concern, the location function has several benefits. Banking online through a smartphone is vulnerable to the usual difficulties of verifying identity, allowing potential identity theft and unauthorized account access. With GPS, the location of a smartphone transaction can at least be matched with a customer's hometown or other usual locations; a large fraudulent transfer ordered from another country can be spotted immediately. There are a number of apps that can help find shops, restaurants, identify driving routes, and more from a user's present location, wherever that may be. Location systems can help parents know where their children are or monitor the movement of disoriented, elderly patients.

GPS is extremely useful; some use stand-alone devices in a car or on a bike, separate from a smartphone, but the trend is to integrate geographical navigation into the digital assistant. As functionality increases, voice directions, traffic conditions, bike paths, hiking trails, restaurants, and other places of business are added, increasing the benefits of GPS. It, too, is becoming a routinely expected smartphone functionality.

Online Shopping and Services

People can use mobile phones for simple to serious online purchases—from books or cosmetics to homes, boats, and cars. Online shopping is changing whole industries, leading to the decline of some brick-and-mortar stores and malls. The convenience of buying without leaving the living room, or even while traveling, is a major change in shopping patterns. What is more, we can shop twenty-four hours a day, every day, and it is easy to find rare items or things no local store carries. Early indications show that using special offers to attract customers is also affecting commerce. A service business might send out messages announcing a discount if people buy during hours when business is normally slow. Restaurants that turn away customers one evening and are empty another can balance revenue with similar off-hour offers.

Information-based management can assist local and national governments, utility services, and countless corporations. Handling individual requests, applications, orders, and administrative services online makes these processes easier for customers at the same time that it improves organizational workflow and personnel efficiency.

Virtual Games

For most, the lure of playing a game is almost irresistible. It is no wonder that, of the first two billion apps downloaded for the iPhone and iPad, 65 percent were games.[72] Online games attract both children and adults. Mobile phones enable us to enjoy the emotional satisfaction of games almost anywhere. But games are not just for entertainment. More and more game-like functions are being integrated into educational tools and apps. These functions engage the learner and stimulate retention as well as interest. Games that use emotional motivators will become major teaching tools in the future.

72　Brian X Chen, "Apple's App Store Hits Six Digits: How Many Apps Do Your Need?," *Gadget Lab*, November 4, 2009. http://www.wired.com/gadgetlab/2009/11/appstore/.

In particular, games where people in geographically different locations can play together will increase in importance and impact. Smartphones are part of this new virtual world that connects people. What does this mean for human intellect? People who used to sit in doctors' waiting rooms, buses, or trains, or in their homes to relax or read a magazine, are now busy with games and communication. Future generations may have much more active minds than previous ones, although some believe that virtual activity discourages deeper thought and contemplation.

News and Magazines

Mobile phones are replacing printed newspapers and magazines, affecting both journalism and advertising. WIC participants conveniently access news via apps and browsers directly on the device. People can also easily read several newspapers from different belief systems, countries, and regions. News-managing apps provide instant news of user interest. Instead of traditional newspapers and magazines that sell print editions and receive revenues from advertisers, the modern news organization will consist of online communities that search for and publish information its members want. The beginnings of such specialized services can be seen in the news alerts that national newspapers send to the mobile phones of registered users. The combination of short messages and images on the phone and longer articles on tablet-style devices, including short videos, is the news service of the future.

Magazine publishers are beginning to realize that their most digitally advanced readers prefer an emagazine version. Within a few months, one of the earlier emagazine publishers, *The New Yorker*, reached a readership of over a hundred thousand people.[73] The digital version of the publication arrives on the reader's device earlier than the print edition can be delivered or is available at a newsstand. On the down side, in its first generation, the electronic version of a

---

73   Jeremy W Peters, "For New Yorker on iPad, Words Are The Thing," *The New York Times,* July 31 2011. http://www.nytimes.com/2011/08/01/business/media/new-yorker-on-ipad-shows-viewers-want-to-read.html?hpw.

magazine is more or less a facsimile of the standard one. Advertising is placed into articles or between articles. Such publishers have not learned from, or have not yet joined the move to, interest-specific advertising. Canceling paper subscriptions and reading magazines on a digital companion makes a lot of sense. It is not difficult to see the next step: magazine subscribers will be a virtual community with specific belief systems, defined by their purchasing preferences and other interests. Advertising will increasingly target such virtual communities.

Radio and TV

Accessing radio and TV broadcasts on a mobile device is much easier than through a radio or TV set, which requires one to be in its presence for listening and viewing. Further, digital broadcasting widens the range of stations a person can listen to. Some ask, "Why would I be interested in listening to a program from another country?" The more exposure people have to other views and information, the more they will be able to question belief systems—their own and others.

Weather

Checking weather information on a smartphone for just about any location, from any other location, at any time, has become routine for millions of people. The "sixth sense" that farmers and others used to have to sense a storm or to forecast weather has been mostly lost. The city dweller used to check TV or radio for general weather information—sometimes several times daily—but only at times scheduled by the station. Now, smartphones and tablets bring anytime access to much more detailed information about local weather. There are hourly forecasts and radar graphs of anticipated precipitation, sun intensity, humidity, air quality, and temperature. It is becoming routine to check weather conditions and forecasts for any travel destination. People also regularly compare the weather their family members, online friends, and colleagues are experiencing in different states or countries. The old question "How's the weather?" has become as specific as "How are you managing with that snowstorm today?" Forecasts will become more precise, more detailed, and more routinely delivered for any location on the planet.

Healthcare and Fitness

Thousands of apps offer information, inspiration, or guidance for health and fitness. They may encourage people to exercise more, lose weight, or simply have fun with a particular sport or exercise program. Fitness apps can also record stats such as how many steps a person takes or the speed of a run or bicycle ride. Apps can support communication-based disease management and provide real-time assistance. Apps or appropriate accessories can collect blood pressure, blood sugar level, and heart rate data, check on asthma symptoms, capture nutritional information, as well as monitor implants. In other words, the device is becoming the dashboard for critical information about our bodies. Now, the patient can routinely and more frequently monitor some functions at home or at work that used to be measured only during visits to the doctor's office. Such home monitoring is still in its embryonic state; apps are not mature, and home monitoring as a virtual healthcare option has not yet been well accepted. But when it is, a whole new world of healthcare will open up.

Ebooks

Book publishers are being hit hard by the digital publishing revolution. Producing a text digitally and publishing it electronically makes sense. It is a major economic improvement. Ebooks cost less to produce and to purchase, and the rapid adoption of ebook devices and apps has produced a new industry and target audience. Traditional publishers fought early arguments that epublishing saves trees, saying that most paper is recycled and that the paper industry is not driven by the publication industry. Also, some point out that energy needed to operate ebook devices and difficulties in discarding old ones affect the environment negatively. Arguments in support of ebooks focus more on their advantages, including quick delivery and free sampling that compete with bookstore browsing, as well as their lower price, which encourages the purchase of more books. But this is only at the surface. Under it is a fundamental change in the way information is read and acquired. The functionalities they offer to look up unfamiliar words on the fly, highlight items of interest, search content, and make organized notes are key developments that are changing our reading habits. Keep in mind that ebooks will evolve over the next decade to become digital information tools. Instead of old-fashioned, isolated reading, book contents will be linked to their sources, to comments by others, and to updates, and they will be indexed so that the reader can follow arguments and subject matter descriptions. I predict that the ebook of 2020 will look quite different from today's: it will better organized for easier reading, use more color images and videos, have improved displays, and provide both meta and core information.

The move from the ebook device to the generic digital portable device in tablet form has already begun. It remains to be seen whether dedicated ebook devices will come up with unique reading and indexing options to attract people to keep buying them. More likely, readers will read their ebooks through apps on generic tablets as well as smartphones, at least in part because they won't have to carry a separate ebook device in addition to a tablet or smartphone. The place of books in daily life will also change. Instead of buying books, keeping them on a shelf in case of a rare reread, and spending time trying to find information in one or another, a home library of digital books frees up space and allows a reader to index and refer to information nearly instantly. The management of the personal digital library will become an important element of knowledge capital.

Here is another prediction: ebooks will be easily updatable. Paper-based books are usually updated through publication of a new edition, if they are updated at all. Authors can update ebooks regularly. This flexibility goes hand in hand with WIC's transparency.

If readers report incorrect or outdated information in a book, the author can update it and automatically send the updated version to readers. Updating software is already a routine procedure for any smartphone or tablet user. The same will become quite common in book publishing.

Sports

The digital companion is the ideal partner for a sports fan who wants to know everything about a favorite team. Whether a player, a spectator, or just a casual exerciser, a user can get relevant information on a mobile device. Current and historic data can be accessed and compared. The range of sports applications is so wide that they could fill a book by themselves. Virtual sports communities will be one of the largest categories of groups with active online communication. A fan will not just go to games, but will want easy access to detailed information about the players and other clubs a team competes with, and to communicate with other fans.

Education

The book and the teacher are being replaced by interactive teaching equipment, educational games, and guiding apps; this trend will increase over the next decade. Early attempts show that games can be used for teaching purposes. Global development of educational apps will serve billions of people who live in rural and nontechnical environments. The smartphone and tablet, along with their apps, will be key in education's future. See Chapter 11 for more information about the impact of WIC on education.

Utilities and Productivity

Many apps are simply programs to make our lives easier. With these, we can manage passwords and membership numbers in one place, find public transportation, take digital notes wherever we are, and scan printed material we might be reading on a plane. These are just some examples of a wide range of tools available on smartphones. The point is that WIC citizens frequently check on new developments and use such programs to better manage their knowledge capital and use it to their best advantage.

Professional Apps

In the first two years of apps, most were designed for personal use. Now the focus is on providing access to professional information through apps that help the engineer, lawyer, academic researcher, clinician, or other professional. Such apps are being integrated into organization information systems. In just a few years, most professionals will likely use apps daily. Over time, professional bodies of knowledge for medicine, law, engineering, and the natural sciences, for instance, will be parsed and prepared for access at the point of work.

The Role of Digital Companions

In the next decades, a new relationship between WIC and human intelligence systems will emerge. The digital companion as knowledge access point and personal trainer will have five new roles that will define WIC capital management:

1. The digital companion, as an extension of our brain's computing power and memory, will give access to huge quantities of information and knowledge to be used at discretion. Since such information will be available to anyone, it will be up to each person to creatively mine the treasures of WIC information for a meaningful life.
2. The digital companion will become a person's keys, wallet, newspaper, geographical guide, teacher, game partner, professional partner, sports pal, fitness trainer, financial advisor,

shopping mall, movie screen, and more. For some, its loss or malfunction may create emotional pain equal to that of losing a close friend or relative. In other words, the digital companion will, over time, become an extension of a person.

3. As a medical support device, the digital companion is likely to monitor health data about a person from birth to death, sending information to a doctor when outside support is needed. The digital companion will be a kind of "seventh sense," routinely coordinating acquisition and integration of health data and alerting a patient or clinician of significant new or different information.

4. Digital companions will guide people in professional, personal, health, recreational, and other areas. Expect that by 2020 the digital companion will be a lifelong teacher and resource in most aspects of life.

5. Over time, digital companions may become digital pets that help overcome loneliness and offer virtual companionship of value, both as a device-friend and through online communities.

Many have perceived machines and computers that look like human beings (i.e., robots) as threatening. This is no surprise: many gods in early religions were like real people, with all the same disruptive motivators. Now we realize that the threat of human displacement comes not so much from robots but rather from the other systems described here that are already being implemented. However, what some perceive as a threat, others perceive as an opportunity to advance individuals, societies, businesses, organizations—even humankind as a whole. Certainly, the digital companion will change a person's meaning, thinking, action, and decision process, as well as the management of information and the self (health, relationships, work, buying habits, and so on).

9

Dangers and Threats to WIC

W IC carries with it a range of threats that can result in loss or distortion of information. Specific hardware improvements or security software help to avoid these, but as one vulnerability is closed, alternatives are sought out and attacked. Just as banks, automobiles, and airplanes can never be 100 percent safe, neither can WIC.

A collapse of information systems would create havoc in our society. If systems are manipulated or shut down by governments, secret services, or terrorists, the damage to industry, commerce, culture, and people could be substantial. Only ten years ago, people imagined how the collapse of computers and the internet would put an end to email and text messages and would create huge data losses for corporations. Now the threat is much greater, since our dependence on computer systems is pervasive. It extends from air traffic control to street lights, from supermarkets to farm operations, from manufacturing to supplies, and more. Most activities and services would cease without computers. Modern societies could not function, and postwar-like conditions would emerge.

The sophistication and complexity of WIC requires vigilance against anything that can harm this informational ecosystem. Dangers include major willful information misrepresentation, shutdowns, collapses, dysfunction, health problems, privacy violations, business interruptions, systems breakdowns, brownouts, loss of connectivity, and criminal effects on people (such as from online robberies). Further, governments may disseminate false information to justify decisions or actions. There could be leakage of proprietary information, information theft (including identity theft), as well as general unavailability of information due to cut off or misdirection of information flow. These dangers are in the league of other major threats, such as wars, the cutoff of energy supplies, bacterial epidemics, nuclear disasters, fatal airborne viruses, breakdowns of power grids, or contamination of air or water.

Computer Hardware and Software

Behavioral health risks are associated with computer use, as noted earlier. Physical inactivity can lead to obesity. Addiction to games or other stimuli can be another health hazard. Long periods of computer work can also cause inflammation in the forearm and wrist areas, including carpal tunnel syndrome. Increased neck, back, and shoulder problems can result from improper sitting and positioning. Eye fatigue, eye irritation, and blurred vision can result from staring at the computer screen. Low-frequency radiation concerns those who believe it causes cancer, while others point out the lack of concrete proof for it.

Hardware failures include computer crashes, disk failures, and system failures that can wipe out valuable information stored on an individual computer. People depend on a working computer and assume it will continue to work. Hard disk crashes occur more often than is generally thought. When a user loses all information in a hardware or software failure, the effect can be as serious as a robbery. Although in most cases much of the information can be recovered, it is still a loss in money, information, and time. Centralized and distributed information storage in the cloud can be safer than local storage and backup. However, cloud computing has its own set of dangers. Everything collapses if connectivity is disrupted. Also, if anything happens to remotely stored information, the damage would be much greater than a loss at the individual computer level. If server farms were destroyed by some unimaginable event, it would be a disaster. Our lives now depend on the knowledge stored on the net and the billions of artificial algorithms built in integrated circuits that govern all global technology-related activities.

Loss of information is one threat. Distortion is another. Computer cookies can distort or misrepresent data, and computer viruses can destroy stored information. Operating systems are vulnerable to hackers and outside interference because they serve millions of users. This has been a particular concern about Microsoft's operating system. It is easier to inject malware into a vast number of computers when they all use the same software. It can bring a whole industry to a halt. A variety of operating systems helps limit this type of potential damage. As competitive systems slowly gain market share, such concerns will lessen.

Deliberate information misrepresentation is as big a threat as system failures. Information can be tampered with or intercepted. For instance, hackers may break into a domain name server (DNS) and hijack or redirect information. They may do it for fun or with criminal intent. A large number of violations come from insiders: people working at ISPs, in computer departments, software development, and related departments inside organizations may break into a system. The public appears to be most concerned with hacking incidents and viruses, although these may not be the most damaging. We hear about data leaks or lost or stolen devices containing personal data, but damage may or may not result. On the other hand, postal workers leave hundreds of pieces of mail unattended on the street daily while delivering to nearby buildings. The possible breach of security if mail is stolen unnoticed is routinely tolerated, but when a disk with data is lost, it makes the evening headlines even if no harm can be demonstrated.

With so many companies involved in the WIC ecosystem, from information service providers to cell phone carriers, millions of insiders could potentially act on motives from financial gain to revenge and hate crimes. Students and others in educational settings make computer hacking a sport. Two Russian hacker communities together have over seventy thousand members.[74] Hacking, viruses, and other malicious software incidents are signs that information is as valuable as money, and consequently must be protected. While some people think these things happen only to large corporations or organizations with public visibility, small organizations can also be targets. My corporate website in Boston was hacked over forty times between 2004 and 2008, fortunately with no detectable harm. But it was a different matter when my internet identity for online banking was stolen and my personal bank account was emptied— twice. Fortunately, the bank replaced the funds. Such incidents occur daily.

Cybercrime is increasing. The US government's attempts to address global cyber security indicate that information guidelines are needed.[75] These efforts will likely be the focus of international politics for years to come, and the creation of international computer and network security standards will require something like a "United Nations for Knowledge Management." Just as national security is defined as the requirement to maintain the survival of the state through economics, power projection, political power, and the exercise of diplomacy, it is important to protect a country's information assets. Penalties for countries and communities that do not adhere to such new standards will likely be developed and imposed.

WIC citizens must protect their knowledge capital not just against hackers who just want to demonstrate that a system is not secure, but also against those who break in to steal identities or money or to use assets illegally. Corporations may try to access competitors' information, and governments, in the name of anti-terrorism and other security measures, may seek information not otherwise available to them. Consider the January 2011 internet shutdown in Egypt. Its internet ecosystem consisted of relatively few internet

---

74   Nelson D Schwarty and Eric Dash, "Thieves Found Citigroup Site an Easy Entry," *The New York Times,* June 14, 2011. http://www.nytimes.com/2011/06/14/technology/14security.html?hp.

75   Helene Cooper, "U.S. Calls for Global Cybersecurity Strategy," *The New York Times,* May 16, 2011.

providers; government officials were able to direct those companies to shut down their systems. Engineers at each provider had to log in to change the traffic configuration of border gateway protocols. This raises the question of the power of internet service providers (ISPs). Although some experts claim that this sort of shutdown could not happen in the United States,[76] others believe the threat exists. Already, Homeland Security and other government agencies are following people's communications and storing them without public accountability or transparency. Government agencies and international groups can potentially disrupt the information network or bring it to a halt. Net neutrality is a goal, but government and corporate interests are stronger than privacy and other public concerns, and they appear at present to be winning.

User agreements also pose a potential threat for abuse. A user installing or updating software has to agree to terms of use that often come in multiple pages of small-print legal language. Most users have no choice but to agree to this legal contract, even if they don't read or understand the whole thing, because declining agreement would mean not having access to the software. A rogue company could place hidden legal terms into such an agreement, and many people would electronically assent. WIC efforts should include finding a way to describe what the user is agreeing to in a few sentences, with an independent organization certifying the appropriate content and value of the proposed agreement.

Information flow governs what information is first accessible. This raises several issues. The first is indexing, which determines whether the information is organized for accessibility or is purposefully hidden. The second is traffic flow. Here a debate about net neutrality should involve lawmakers, companies, and user representatives. In theory, all information packages should be handled equally, but capacity problems occur because some apps and users (for instance, internet phone applications or VoIP) take up more bandwidth. Is the internet moving to a system similar to that of road traffic, where one can take a fast toll road or use a slower free one? Keep in mind that societies, communities, corporations, and others

---

76   Jennifer Valentino-DeVries, "How Egypt Killed the Internet," *The Wall Street Journal,* January 28, 2011.

prefer to promote access to information that conforms to their belief system and to obscure or make inaccessible opposing views. Threats of information manipulation do not just affect indexing, but also the reliability of content, sites, platforms, interoperability, and modes of communication. Here, commercial and political interests sometimes clash with principles of free information and knowledge distribution. The Age of Enlightenment brought attempts toward equality and fair treatment of all people. The new era of WIC will seek fair distribution of and access to information for all.

Mobile Devices

Mobile devices connect wirelessly to the internet and to each other. This brings an additional range of threats. Loss of connectivity can threaten the mobile sections of WIC. Broadband and Wi-Fi connectivity are as important to the advanced state of WIC as oxygen is for human survival. Ensuring connectivity in remote rural areas is a concern, as are potential urban overloads that cause brownouts (loss of connectivity due to overuse).

Mobile devices function as small computers on which valuable information is stored and accessed. The loss of such a device not only can create difficulties, it can enable others to misuse valuable proprietary information stored in it or accessible through it. Therefore, systems must be put in place that require special passwords or biometric keys for access. Through location services, devices can be geographically located if lost or stolen, and information can even be remotely wiped (deleted) from them.

All computers (and most other electronic devices) emit some electromagnetic radiation, one of the key forces on this planet. Electromagnetism may cause one computer to interfere with another (and the user may hear sudden feedback on electrical devices). But we don't know all the effects of electromagnetism on information stored or processed on electrical devices. Around the turn of the century, electromagnetic interference could cause other sensitive devices, particularly medical ones, to malfunction. For this reason, most hospitals banned cell phones in treatment areas.[77] Since then, cell phone makers have reduced electromagnetic output until interference is so minimal that it does not affect most medical devices. Further, means for managing electromagnetic interference have been developed and are also widely used, so mobile devices are routine in healthcare settings. Conversely, the airline industry still forbids their use while planes are taking off and landing.

The purported health hazards of mobile devices have been circulated for years, including rumors about brain cancer. Fear is one of the strongest emotional motivators, and it creates lasting belief systems. In 1992, cell phone user Susan Elen Reynard was diagnosed with malignant astrocytoma, a brain cancer that seems to occur in about six thousand American adults each year.[78] Her husband was convinced that the shape, size, and position of the tumor corresponded with his wife's phone when held against her left ear. But the husband's suit against the cell phone manufacturer and the carrier was rejected by the Florida Circuit Court in 1995 because of "uncertainty of the evidence...[and] the speculative scientific hypotheses and [incomplete] epidemiological studies."[79] Five years later, the neurologist Christopher Newman sued Motorola, claiming that he had developed brain cancer after using his cell phone for an estimated 343 hours.[80] Again, his case was dismissed for lack of evidence. Compare the fear of cell phones with the malignant influence of tobacco smoking on lung cancer. First suspected in the 1930s, it took thirty years from the first legal case until prejudices could be overcome and the effect of smoking on people's health could be fully established. Meanwhile, tobacco smoking persisted, and it continues today.

Cell phone radiation is decreasing due to smaller units and less power use. Therefore, even if cancer could occasionally be caused

---

77   Claudia Tessier and C Peter Waegemann, *Electromagnetic Compatibility* (Boston: Mobile Healthcare Alliance, 2004).

78   Siddharta Mukherjee, "Do Cell Phones Cause Cancer?" *The New York Times,* April 13, 2011.

79   Ibid.

80   Marguerite Reardon, "Cell phone radiation: Harmless or health risk?" *CNET News,* May 31, 2011. http://news.cnet.com/8301-30686_3-20066842-266. html?tag=mncol;txt.

in the 1990s, today's devices are much more refined, their cases stronger, and their power use reduced. In other words, the thin, small mobile phone of today cannot be compared with the crude phones available before the turn of the century.

Cancer experts at the University of Pittsburgh Cancer Institute issued a warning in 2008 urging faculty and staff to limit their use of mobile phones because of possible cancer risk.[81] In early 2011, a study by the National Institutes of Health showed that glucose metabolism increased in the area of the brain when a phone and its antenna were held close to the head while the phone was on.[82] But again, no health risks were found. The World Health Organization's International Agency for Research on Cancer confirmed in June 2011 that there are possible health hazards with mobile phones, but also that none have been proven.[83] The industry keeps within the US limit of 1.6 watts per kilogram specific absorption rate (SAR), and many mobile phones emit well below that—in some cases, only half that level. In Europe, where the concern is greater, the official cap is 2 watts per kilogram. So, what is the bottom line? With more cell phones in use than cars or TVs, mobile devices and their limited radiation will be part of our lives, whether we like it not. Select a mobile phone with a low emission rate. Most radiation is emitted with voice functions; using a speaker microphone, headset, and texting features can reduce radiation exposure. Watch the signal strength: fewer bars mean that the device must emit more radiation to get a signal to a tower. Special care should be taken when children use mobile phones. They appear more naturally inclined to use texting, so this should be encouraged over voice communications. Neither adults nor children should carry mobile phones close to the body when calls come in or when placing calls. Men should not carry

81   W David Gardner, "Cancer Expert Issues Warning On Cell Phone Risks," *InformationWeek*, July 24, 2008. http://www.informationweek.com/news/mobility/business/209600447.

82   Nora D Volkow, et al., "Effects of Cell Phone Radiofrequency Signal Exposure on Brain Glucose Metabolism," *Journal of the American Medical Association*, 2011; 305 (8): 808–813. http://jama.ama-assn.org/content/305/8/808.short.

83   "Electromagnetic fields and public health: mobile phones," World Health Organization, June 2011. http://www.who.int/mediacentre/factsheets/fs193/en/.

mobile phones on their belts to avoid any radiation effects on their genitals.[84]

One drawback of mobile devices is their appetite for energy. Battery solutions to date have been less than ideal. Batteries that absorb solar or motion energy could help.

Cloud Computing

Cloud computing allows software functionality and information to be stored remotely in a network of processing systems. For individual users and companies, the cloud brings advantages in costs and maintenance. It is easier to make information and software secure at dedicated locations located near energy production sites and equipped with security features. This reduces the potential problems from a failure in the electricity grid. With information distributed across multiple locations and computers, it cannot be destroyed by an attack or operational problem at a single computer. Software only needs to be updated at the remote network rather than multiple times at individual computer installations, reducing expenses. Cloud computing offers more flexibility in implementation and mobility: people can log into the knowledge base from anywhere. Disaster recovery is also more easily done in cloud systems.

But cloud computing also has big risks. Information can be inaccessible with the loss of connectivity, which depends on an ISP, a telecommunications carrier, a network of Wi-Fi spots, or other connections. Second is a lack of control over information. There is also the issue of security. A "standard" cloud computing agreement may not offer users the security level they desire or need, or the cloud company may charge more for more sophisticated and effective security.

---

84   Devra Davis, *Disconnect: The Truth About Cell Phone Radiation, What the Industry Has Done to Hide It, and How to Protect Your Family* (New York, Dutton, Kindle Edition, 2010), 1956.

Security and Privacy

Security and privacy issues, of course, are not limited to cloud computing. However, some suspect that government or other organizations will have easier access to private information when it is stored in remote dedicated servers. A person or company that fears disclosure of information is well advised to think twice about cloud computing. At a minimum, special encryption and other security measures must be implemented to ensure that owners with these concerns are notified every time their information is accessed. The misuse of personalized data is of particular concern in the areas of finance, health information, and behavioral data.

In the last fifty years, information technology and computerization have brought greater efficiencies in the management of customer, membership, client, prospect, patient, consumer, insurance and publication subscriber, and licensee data (i.e., drivers' licenses). Without these databases about people's habits and their information consumption, our society and economy would function very differently. Many people aren't aware of the web of personal information around each individual. Your doctor can know past illnesses from your electronic medical record, your automobile insurance agent can quickly check your driving history, a bank officer can check your credit history, a law officer can reconstruct your movements from public surveillance cameras, and public records can document any violations of law, as well as the properties that you own.

Now, the internet and the whole WIC system go a step further. Computers identify keywords from your correspondence to advertise related products. Cookies planted in your computer may use algorithms for information processing without your awareness, authorization, or desire. Inappropriate information typed (willfully or by mistake) cannot be deleted and can be accessed. Your opinions may be accessed, broadcast, and used against you. Systems can identify where you are or where you have been (both physically and virtually). Every aspect of your personal taste is potentially discoverable (including in the most sensitive areas of sexuality and belief systems). Your purchasing profile tells details about your nutrition and favorite products. These kinds of information compose a comprehensive picture of who you are. There is no hiding place.

Can this trend be resisted or controlled? I believe that the genie is out of the bottle and that the trend cannot be reversed. Fighting for privacy is a quixotic battle that is not winnable. Too many systems are in place that cannot be turned off. And, the same people who want privacy in one or more areas do not want it in others, thus complicating its implementation and monitoring. Of equal importance are liabilities related to privacy.

Traditional views of privacy are in decline.[85] At the same time, the interest in transparency is growing. As mentioned earlier, there is a general move toward transparency in government, corporate, and personal information. Transparency in society and information systems implies openness, communication, and accountability. Transparency could become the desired next step for knowledge systems in our society. Imagine that people, governments, and organizations become accountable, transparent, and open in their objectives and actions. Imagine that organizational insiders (employees, government workers, and others) would have to worry if they behave inappropriately or unethically, because they are likely to be exposed. Imagine that no one can use power to hide, manipulate, or misuse information.

Organizations need to take appropriate measures to address the potential leakage of adverse information. While internal policies may restrict them officially, they may not be easily enforceable. It is important to train all people in an organization to create and document only appropriate information, whether in email, on the company website, or elsewhere. Inappropriate language or statements expressed over the phone were generally not captured in the past, but they often are now. So are text messages, email, and internal notes. Any recorded information can be used against an organization or individual.

---

85 "Over time, users have become less likely to express concern about the amount of information available about them online." *Pew Internet Report*, May 26, 2010. http://www.pewinternet.org/Reports/2010/Reputation-Management/Part-2/Attitudes-and-Actions.aspx.

The Worst Dangers

Three worst-case scenarios depict what could affect WIC. The first is that a single entity, perhaps a government or other organization, somehow takes control of the WIC system. It could manipulate information, make some information inaccessible, and influence worldwide information access and opinion building. This scenario transforms people into tools of a belief system. It could dramatically change our civilization. Therefore, it is most important to guard the openness and transparency of WIC. Organizations that monitor privacy and data protection should monitor WIC systems to ensure that they are not hijacked.

The second scenario would be the unintended collapse of cloud computing, wireless communication—or computing in general. Overuse could result in brownouts that overwhelm the wireless communication infrastructure. Or environmental influences, such as strong magnetic fields, satellite failure, software platform failure, or something currently unknown, could make computing inoperable. This scenario could erase all digitally stored information (from books to software). People and organizations could not function, as if after a nuclear war. Those who survive would have to build a knowledge base from scratch.

The third scenario would be the result of intense cyber warfare. Governments, secret service powers, or other groups or organizations could cripple each other's WIC infrastructure, deliberately causing dysfunctions as in scenario two.

Knowledge through information is our capital. It must be managed and protected. The above scenarios describe threats that are as serious as a limited nuclear war and potentially more damaging than planetary disasters, a global airborne killer virus, food shortages, or the effects from global warming.

Misconceptions

The media have promoted several misconceptions, influencing general belief systems about new technologies. The media said "don't trust the internet," "don't trust the computer," and "don't trust the mobile phone." I participated in an early investigation of the common sentiment that patients should not seek medical information on the internet for fear it was incorrect. It was very costly to learn that, in fact, very little medical information on the internet was incorrect. Compared with the discrepancy of medical knowledge between countries, internet medical knowledge was not out of line. Further, unlike books and other print materials, information on the internet can easily and quickly be corrected and updated. This is also true of other projects like Wikipedia, where corrections are made continually. The attitude that cell phones are untrustworthy sources of medical information is both toxic and misleading. The size of the phone does not limit the information it can provide. At the end of the twentieth century, people often blamed faulty output on computers, but more people now realize that human input or instructions determine a computer's product. As the saying goes, "garbage in, garbage out."

Millions of emails are sent and delivered daily without incident, and email is safer than postal mail, which has been historically subject to regular violations. Still, many organizations insist on transmitting signed documents by "snail" mail or fax because of outdated legal advice. The same applies to texting, considered unsafe by many organizations. While it is true that a text message may sometimes be delayed for hours, this is a carrier problem that is corrected as more data transmission capacity is added. Further, where greater "safety" is required or desired, secure text messaging apps are available.

Although substantial risks exist in WIC, it is important to realize that major organizations are striving to make the new information system secure and safe as well as accessible and simple to use.

10

Managing Information and Knowledge Capital

The symbiosis of technology-based knowledge, computing, and communication systems with human interactions is real, and many people get excited about the wealth of information and knowledge that WIC makes available. However, WIC, by itself, will not change people's lives. A traditional library benefits those who seek books and information greatly, but many never take advantage of it. Now, WIC offers the same advantages (and more) to anyone, at any time, in any place. It also makes many other daily functions easier and more convenient: online shopping; online banking; online local, state, and federal government interactions. In almost every area of our lives, WIC facilitates access to information. Just as the invention of the automobile gave people new life experiences through individual travel more convenient than stagecoach or train, WIC offers new advantages to those who use it. While many of the new opportunities that WIC offers will take years to become mainstream, a great number of people already rely on either the computer and/or a digital companion. For some, this reliance approaches a form of dependence they only recognize when they have difficulties with (or lose) their mobile phone.

Nevertheless, WIC also has negative aspects. Organizing and managing communication is one of the top challenges. For example, these are disruptive technologies that require different time management, because it is no longer easy to be unavailable on weekends, at night, or even on vacation. The new WIC citizen must manage text, email, chat, and other communication by determining which messages require a response and which have priority. Further, while the trend toward greater transparency brings many advantages, it also raises privacy issues. Someone who appreciates the transparency of knowing why a bank does not approve a loan request may not appreciate that his or her financial status and dealings also have become more transparent.

More disruptive, and potentially disastrous, is WIC's impact on businesses. As buyers use online offers, some businesses experience major losses, and some cannot survive. In turn, many people will lose their jobs. Businesses under pressure will try to stay competitive by laying off employees. Unemployment is a major consequence of computerization and net technologies, but at the same time, it leads to new jobs and new opportunities.

The New Information Business Model

Traditionally, each society has had a system for transporting written communications. In modern times, this has typically been in the form of a national postal system. When the introduction of email reduced the cost of sending communications, a quiet revolution took place as more and more users chose communication by email over the postal delivery system. When the amount of spam mail became a nuisance, email providers introduced spam filters, or users moved to text or social media communication. These new communication tools also reduced communicating by telephone, a significant social change.

Since the days of the printing press, business models have bundled the cost of the medium with the value of the information it communicates. Ebooks and emagazines, for example, have far lower production and transportation costs than traditional publishing, thus creating a new business model for the industry. People can even rent digital books instead of buying a digital or print version. In the movie business model, most films for home viewing are not bought, but rented. In the music business, record and CD production is being replaced by less costly electronic downloads.

These examples indicate that the new business model will be selling access to information, or in other words, its usage. Rather than buying books, CDs, and DVDs and keeping them in living rooms or libraries, WIC people will access them for a small fee. This new information business model will be disruptive in several ways.

Job Losses

A major restructuring in the world of WIC is the move from physical labor to knowledge work. People have a long history of finding replacements to do physical work: using animals such as donkeys, camels, and oxen to transport heavy goods; enslaving people; using wind and water to create power to process grain, and so on. A wide range of mechanical devices also assisted. The extraction of fossil fuels enabled steam engines, motors, and electric machines. The amount of labor developed countries outsource to machines is not always recognized. In factories, on farms, and in construction, the work of several people can be done by one powerful mechanical device. Automated soil cultivation, planting, irrigation, harvesting, haymaking, and milking replaced farm workers of the past. If work can be streamlined and organized into repetitive processes, a machine can and will do it more economically. As machines "learn," some will become robots that do not need a human to run them. Robots can work 24/7, do not require "breaks" or any time off, and they recover initial implementation expenses in a few years. What will be the consequences of robots and machines replacing physical labor and semi-knowledge labor? Does this mean that there will be too many workers for fewer jobs? In the short run, it may seem to be the case, but arguably there will be a shift toward a different role for people in our society as "information jobs" increase.

WIC is crossing borders and national barriers. The next system that creates jobs may not come from the United States, but from China, India, Brazil, or a country we may not think of as a breeding ground for new information systems. Information technology skills, innovation, and international marketing are the keys to success and job growth.

The 2010–2011 Global Information Technology Report issued by INSEAD and the World Economic Forum states, "While changing the way individuals live, interact, and work, ICT [information and communication technology] has also proven to be a key precondition for enhanced competitiveness and economic and societal modernization, as well as an important instrument for bridging economic and social divides and reducing poverty."[86] Future economic competition among national industries, as well as government-directed economic measures, will be heavily influenced by information technologies. This will have a dual impact. On one hand, information technology will lead to a decrease in jobs in many industries as organizations become more efficient with new systems and devices. On the other hand, economic growth will increasingly depend on growth in the field of information technology. National politics, such as healthcare strategies, depend largely on the ability to achieve savings through information technology. Poverty, both in the United States and abroad, could potentially be reduced through information technologies.[87] The competitiveness of economies depends on their conditions for information industries: national rules and laws concerning WIC activities, the encouragement of communities, the creation of digital highways, connectiv-

---

86   Robert Greenhill, "Preface," *The Global Information Technology Report 2010-2011—Transformations 2.0* (Geneva: World Economic forum and INSEAD, 2011), 7. http://www3.weforum.org/docs/WEF_GITR_Report_2011.pdf.

87   Torbjörn Frediksson, "The Growing Possibilities of Information and Communication Technologies for Reducing Poverty," *The Global Information Technology Report 2010-2011—Transformations 2.0* (Geneva: World Economic forum and INSEAD, 2011), 69. http://www3.weforum.org/docs/WEF_GITR_Report_2011.pdf.

ity in remote rural areas, brainstorming centers that stimulate new ideas, and cultural support for information technology (particularly in the fourth estate: the media and press).

We are in a race toward the most important industry change of our time. The Global Information Technology Report cites many measurable components that enable the growth of information technology in a country. Two issues need to be addressed. One is the enabling environment; the other concerns users and usage. Environmental components include market environment, political and regulatory conditions for new companies and general digital information use, the digital infrastructure, individual readiness, business readiness and implementation, and government readiness. The usage component has three categories: the states of individual, business, and government usage. Ranking 138 countries in each of these fields, the report gives an overview of national developments.

- In market environment, venture capital availability is measured. The top five countries are Hong Kong, Norway, Singapore, Finland, and Luxemburg. The United States is ranked 13th, Canada 19th, Australia 12th, and the United Kingdom 38th.
- Sweden, Iceland, Norway, Finland, and Switzerland lead in availability of the latest technology. The United States is in 7th place, Canada 14th, and the United Kingdom is 15th.
- Sweden, Singapore, Estonia, Denmark and Norway have the best laws for enabling information technologies through electronic commerce, digital signatures, and consumer protection in online businesses. New Zealand is 8th, Canada 10th, Australia 11th, US 15th, and UK 16th.
- As for the percentage of total population covered by a mobile network signal in 2010, nineteen countries had reached the 100 percent mark, including Hong Kong, Israel, Chile, and Switzerland. The UK is in 33rd place, the US in 40th, and Canada in 48th.[88]

---

88   Ibid.

Regarding the last topic, coverage by a mobile network signal, I should note that it is more important to measure 3G and 4G availability than just mobile coverage, because the level of service matters. For instance, India has wide regions that have only basic voice or text services. To enable WIC access, a higher level of telecommunication services is needed.

Knowledge Society

The possibility of some countries leapfrogging from an agricultural state to that of a knowledge society and knowledge economy is fascinating. However, the developments of the industrial age, with its manual factories for assembly cannot be bypassed. In China and many other countries, industrial developments are partly on the path toward the knowledge society. The challenge is how to transfer knowledge on a large scale to populations that are illiterate in the traditional sense, so that they can be brought to a level of WIC literacy that enables them to provide value in the knowledge economy of the future.

Over the last hundred years, a new professional category has evolved: the semi-knowledge worker, who routinely supports an information device, such as a typewriter, calculator, or computer, by inputting data the device cannot yet capture by itself. In other words, the semi-knowledge worker is not involved in creative information processes but rather facilitates the information processing machine by feeding or manipulating data. In today's economy, the semi-knowledge worker is the data entry person, bank teller, or accountant. However, automated processes are slowly replacing semi-knowledge workers, e.g., ATMs are replacing some bank tellers.

In contrast to semi-knowledge workers, the knowledge worker solves problems, designs concepts, creates economic value through business solutions, and develops systems that maximize information processing. Information processing and communication systems also have an impact on professions, such as medicine, law, and education. For instance, legal assistants who helped attorneys research their cases are slowly being replaced by legal search systems.

In summary, three technology developments are causing people to lose their jobs: increased automation and mechanization, where increasingly sophisticated machines and devices replace physical labor; semi-knowledge workers are replaced by automated systems; and information-processing systems are replacing support personnel for knowledge workers. Through WIC's potential, many corporate structures of knowledge workers, such as hospitals, law firms, libraries, colleges, and universities, will change their processes and business models, also leading to a reduction in employees.

Let's put this in perspective: Instead of exuberantly praising technological developments or lamenting their consequent painful changes, we must prepare ourselves for maximizing their benefits. Knowledge capital can enhance personal power. It can help make someone more competitive, better able understand information, and have greater insight into life. Knowledge capital is available to those who want to acquire and use it. Just as financial capital opportunities can be missed if a person does not strive to recognize and respond to circumstances, knowledge capital, now suddenly available to the majority through the internet and other developments, must be sought, acquired, managed, and treasured.

Personal Knowledge Capital

When people hear the term "capital," they think of financial capital. But labor is also a form of capital: people could market their physical work. In the past, people's ability to do hard physical work declined as they aged: eventually, their labor capital was spent and they had to be subsidized by family, insurance, a union, or the state. In general, western societies have largely moved from physical labor to office work that usually involves information handling. Today's knowledge worker may continue to work well past the traditional retirement age.

In the not too distant future, the terms *knowledge disorder*, *WIC dysfunctionality*, and *information disorder* will describe limited abilities to combine brainpower with the knowledge of WIC. It may be acceptable for an elderly person to be dysfunctional in managing advanced technologies in the same way it was when a person of a certain age couldn't do labor-intensive work. Few others will be able to, or want to, avoid being a part of WIC. Increasingly, knowledge capital will define one's life.

Hundreds of years ago, the main social role was growing food. A minority served in trade, government, education, law, and medicine. Today, automatic devices can potentially replace most employees (and be more reliable). However, a person's knowledge is always of value to society, to a cause, or to a company that needs it.

Thus, the new field of information and knowledge management is emerging around the future's most important function. Knowledge, information, and belief systems define a person. Knowledge is valuable capital that needs maintenance and expansion. It is not limited to one's formal education; it is a life-long activity. The most valuable knowledge is usually learned later in life. Compare your knowledge base to a piece of land. If you don't maintain it, it will soon be overgrown. If you don't organize your knowledge, your knowledge base will soon be filled with trivia: information that may satisfy some emotional motivator but is not useful for a successful and meaningful life. Therefore, it is beneficial to make an effort to understand one's strengths (knowledge that can be employed) and weaknesses (missing knowledge that would be beneficial to have). Knowledge can be categorized within personal intelligence systems: knowledge required for a job, for recreation, for financial matters, for sports, for politics, for news, for art, for computer use, and for many other intelligence systems. It should also be acknowledged that people often consume information that is widely available through the popular press but is of little or no value as knowledge capital.

Understanding the strengths and weaknesses of your knowledge base must begin with an inventory of the information you have acquired. This may sound overwhelming, but you can easily identify some of its building blocks. Starting with childhood, identify information that helped create the unique "you." This could prove to be quite enlightening. You should also examine your formal education beyond a diploma from a specific school. What focus did your school have? Which teachers had an impact, positive or negative? Did early praise lead to an interest in a professional field later? Consider creating an informational autobiography. Identify key points when you acquired opinions or when you found a field you were interested in. All this information formed you as a person. You differ from others in the way you look and dress, but that is just the surface. The real distinction is in your interests, motivations, knowledge, prejudices, opinions, and your information-based skills. It is important to address knowledge and information apart from emotional motivators. When people make mistakes, and decisions lead to negative results, they often blame events or other people. Managing your knowledge capital requires an objective look at your own decision-making processes.

Evaluating your knowledge capital is a life-long quest. You are chasing a moving target. But it can illustrate your strengths and weaknesses for knowledge work. The challenge is how to maximize the benefits from your information capital: to find a job or to use your knowledge to create value in nontraditional activities (create or join a skill cooperative, for instance).

Participating in WIC depends not only on a person's willingness and ability, but also on the technical infrastructure of a region or country. This does not only distinguish developed countries from undeveloped countries. Even in the most developed, different levels of WIC infrastructure influence the management of knowledge capital.

Traditional social class structure is based on station in life, financial capital, educational degrees, and special privileges. However, many of these class features are fading. For instance, a high school diploma does not guarantee the knowledge capital to find a meaningful job, nor does a college degree or even a PhD. A new definition is forming that will detail what knowledge enables people in the world of WIC to provide value, either in a structured job or otherwise. I propose that educational bodies make it a priority to help people manage their knowledge systems.

Managing Knowledge Capital in Organizations

Companies, organizations, and governments should identify their knowledge capital both at the general and employee level and as linked to their missions and values. Business intelligence has three challenges. First, all information silos and their purposes must be identified. In most instances, some of these databases should be consolidated. Their information should be analyzed in order to improve efficiency and productivity and to reduce costs and the speed of research, i.e., the time it takes to extract information from various sources. Information capital must be protected from leakage, and new information must be added as companies continually analyze the marketplace.

Second, information assets must go through a process of analysis. Many organizations have initiated enterprise intelligence and business analytics projects, but often these are done in a piecemeal fashion. It is not sufficient to understand an organization's history concerning processes and information assets. Predictive analytics should involve asset identification, data mining, statistical analysis, forecasting, and predictive modeling for each department.

The third challenge involves new procedures that enable users to maximize the value of information. Companies must encourage employees to exchange information within departments and throughout the organization and to be openly creative rather than work in isolated cubicles. The use of mobile devices should be customized within an organization, particularly for ease of use, efficient information access, and company security. At the same time, knowledge capital must be protected against competitors' efforts to learn about technical, marketing, strategic, and management intentions, since these can be decisive in the marketplace. Long-term knowledge capital management is sometimes of a higher value than short-term financial gain. It may be tempting to allow a subcontractor to widen its expertise, but this can simply create a new competitor, as the case of Dell versus ASUS demonstrates.[89] ASUS, a contractor of Dell manufactured parts, offered more and more sophisticated parts until it started marketing a full computer in direct competition. "Knowledge enabling" must be a consideration when doing business with subcontractors and others.

A corporate knowledge asset or knowledge capital manager should support the chief information officer of any company or organization. The duties of an information officer concern the introduction of new technologies, efficient information flow, communication systems, integrated information processing systems, safe storage applications, and user access of information; in contrast, the knowledge asset manager is responsible for identification of intelligence systems and internal knowledge that enable an organization to succeed and prosper. The goals of organizational knowledge management should be:

- Management of the organizational image (in the press and public view)
- Transparency for the organization while also protecting asset knowledge
- Identification and management of organizational asset knowledge
- Ongoing evaluation of asset knowledge: identifying knowledge needs and filling them
- Enabling and promoting new information that can support organizational goals.

Such goals differ from the traditional efforts of a human resource department that manages people as resources. Although the term *human resources* implies that it is mainly the knowledge of employees that represents their value, its focus is more on employee performance and employment matters, such as salary, hours, and benefits, than on anyone's unique knowledge contribution. In contrast,

---

89   Steve Denning, "Why Amazon Can't Make a Kindle in the USA" *Forbes*, August 17, 2011. http://www.forbes.com/sites/stevedenning/2011/08/17/why-amazon-ca,nt-make-a-kindle-in-the-usa/.

knowledge management concerns itself with employees' knowledge and their best use of it.

Information/Knowledge Management at the National Level

Government roles have evolved during the last decades of the twentieth century. Globalization, first through air travel, then through communication (telephone, fax, internet, and WIC), is influencing national goals and priorities. Making life better through improved economic conditions and providing transparency and freedom have reached a new prominence in national considerations. Conditions for knowledge acquisition through education and WIC access have become measurements for future employment, competitiveness, and industrial success. The move from labor-intensive economies focused on productivity to information-intensive economies focused on value creation will be the challenge of the next decades.

Under these conditions, two roles are of particular importance to governments. The first concerns the general state of knowledge and information management. This includes the public's acceptance of new information and communication technologies. When I compare countries' newspaper reports about an information technology issue, I see differences ranging from pro-technology comments to "not sure, be careful" or even "don't trust the internet" and "never use Wikipedia." Much of this negative attitude stems from a distrust of computers and the internet, as well as of their users. It is important to create a national information climate that assures citizens of WIC's advantages while it identifies, describes, and protects against its potential dangers.

Government's second role in a WIC world is creating maximum conditions for the appropriate industries, which in turn will create new jobs. For years, it has been recognized that information and communication technologies (especially in virtual and social media) can become the driving force for new employment and economic benefits. The INSEAD analysis, which ranked countries on factors that could make the most of new WIC conditions for citizens and industry, does not explain why Sweden, Finland, Singapore, and Switzerland were ranked as the top four in ICT enabling and the United States fifth. The most influential developments, from PCs, software, and indexing (Google, Bing, etc.) to smartphones (iPhone, Android, etc.) and tablets (iPad, Kindle Fire, etc.), could lead one to argue that the US holds first place in creating the new disruptive technologies that form the basis for the knowledge society. On the other hand, Germany, one of the leading industrial nations with strengths in technology production and innovation, is in 13th place despite its social plus points. The German culture encourages people to mistrust new information developments, suspects leading companies (such as Google) of evil, focuses on data protection rather than transparency, and encourages consumers to be in a state of constant alert. Imagine a country (such as Germany) that is heavily dependent on automobile production and consumption constantly reminding drivers and buyers that the automobile is one of the most dangerous devices, that thousands of people die or get severely injured by cars, and that using automobiles should be avoided.

Consider the changes that WIC will bring over the next decades. The importance of where a person is born and lives, and of access to traditional education, will diminish as people gain access to information that enables them to learn and create personal knowledge capital anywhere, anytime. This personal knowledge capital will enable everyone to find a valued place in society. Granted, it is far too early to realize the democratization of opportunity that WIC will enable. Just as the need for a national highway system was the impetus for industrialization, so information technology is the pathway to the new information age. Thus, national priorities should focus on the availability of internet connections and maximizing conditions for people to become knowledge workers. Billions of people who previously were shut out will be able to participate in future competitive and creative information societies. While the first decade of the twenty-first century has experienced the transfer of industrial labor to low-cost countries, the second and third decades will experience creativity and inventions from newly knowledge-enabled people throughout the world.

WIC will enable vast developments in our global economy, which will require adjustments at every level. The solution must be the information infrastructure combined with knowledge to create value. Governments should create jobs, but not only through general stimulus packages or tax policies; they should provide coaching and education to guide people into new ways to contribute to the economy and to the benefit of others.

The current goal of producing more and more goods will lead to a crisis. A new target must be introduced: that of producing information-based value. For example, instead of sending sophisticated equipment to undeveloped regions, it may be better to send information content through simple devices—like mobile devices with apps in the local language or dialect—that guide villagers toward basic medical help and improved living conditions. Additionally, information available to the developed world must be restructured and designed in ways that help anyone to become a part of WIC. A level of equality can be achieved with information transfer.

For example, many people are concerned that the world's population is growing so fast that it will exceed food supply within this century. We need to transfer information about how to grow food according to climate, soil, skills, and water resources to all corners of the world. The challenge to the information industry will be to develop simple information programs that will help countries where food is in short supply. New business models will arise to sell information content. Content providers may share the future profits. Apps may be sold for just a few cents to tens of thousands of users. Apps may use pictures and videos to communicate to those who are illiterate.

Further, will our society understand and take steps to transition from violence to information-based conflict resolution? Human development has perpetuated the animalistic trend of resolving conflicts through violence. Clubs, spears, and bows and arrows gave way to knives and swords; then we blasted the enemy with guns and bombs, and now we threaten chemical warfare and bioterrorism. In the second half of this century of global travel, global economies, and multinational politics, will armies be reduced or eliminated? Will transparency extend to identifying every nuclear weapon with an RFID to monitor its location? Can such weapons be protected against terrorists and other enemies? Can we learn as citizens of WIC that conflicts can be settled better in debates or "information warfare" without killing innocent people? The growth of global information capital requires that we think about these issues.

Capital is the resource that enables people and countries to compete and succeed. It has many forms: financial, political, social, health, and knowledge. The latter is the most important asset we have, and it must be carefully managed if we are to thrive and succeed individually and collectively.

11

The Future

History has shown that development happens in spurts. Periods full of inventions and new developments are followed by times when they get integrated into new devices and meaningful use. Who could have forecast how the wheel would change lives and society over thousands of years? Nor could one easily predict the impact of electricity. When the first eyeglasses were invented at the end of the 13th century, no one could imagine that they would lead to the microscope. By 1930, the first electronic microscope achieved a magnification of 400 times; by the end of the twentieth century, high-resolution microscope imaging could magnify 50 million times. This has led to discoveries that help us understand viruses, nanobes, and other microorganisms, some far more dangerous than what we think of as our ancestors' enemies (bears, lions, tigers, and so on). Similarly, it is important to keep in mind that it is difficult to foresee the details and extent of the impact that WIC might have. As we speculate about the impact of WIC through the twenty-first century and beyond, we must acknowledge that unforeseen consequences are likely.

WIC's systematic, structural, personal, and societal changes will be disruptive. Earlier, I described changes in publishing. Many other areas also show signs of dramatic change, including education, government, the role of advertising in the economy, and scientific research.

New communication methods and access to WIC will provide more than a thousandfold the knowledge of the traditional individual teacher in a classroom. Thus, the learning process will move from the schoolroom to a virtual space in which the teacher serves as a virtual coach. Monitoring the learning process remotely, educators will focus on teaching students to understand context. But here is the danger: In the world of WIC, traditional authorities (school boards, school superintendents, principals, even teachers) will lose control over learning materials. As ideologists recognize that teachers, educational processes, and educational material will be used to create belief systems, there will be a political struggle over teaching agendas.

The cost of education will come down. This will affect all educational institutions. App prices for mobile phones start in a very low price range ($0.99 to $2.99), and access to high value online courses will be available to students for very low fees. Take as an example the online course on artificial intelligence that Stanford University offered for free in fall 2011.[90] Over a hundred thousand students enrolled. Most of them might readily have paid $1 to $3 for the course, making it a significant revenue source.

The challenge for educational institutions will be to move from standard classroom teaching to offering courses that are of interest and benefit to large numbers of students across vast distances. No longer will an education system's student population be geographically limited. With its current seven billion people, the world has the marketing potential for attracting students globally. Specialized courses in developed countries may have thousands of online students. Value will also be created in courses that help people in

---

90   Aaron Saenz, "100,000+ Sign Up For Stanford's Open Class on Artificial Intelligence. Classes with 1 Million+ Next?" *Singularity Hub*, August 18, 2011. http://singularityhub.com/2011/08/18/100000-sign-up-for-stanfords-open-class-on-artificial-intelligence-classes-with-1-million-next/.

undeveloped areas to manage health issues, raise more food, and increase their quality of life. "Basic courses," say, for undeveloped countries, will be created with images and video instruction in local languages. Local networks will enable one person in the village to project the course information onto a wall so that many people can participate. Thousands of people will develop materials that will intrigue and teach. Some will teach body hygiene, others digital hygiene, and still others will teach such topics as basic agricultural material, foundations of literacy, health, social issues, and more.

I predict that in the near future there will be thousands of educational apps available. Entrepreneurs, rather than colleges or universities, will design most educational courses. Easy-to-learn apps will be designed for every possible area of knowledge. The ease of presenting information will lead to a competition in best practices, but the content itself will be subject to a WIC-based educational program that provides guidelines in an open and transparent process. It may take some time for these educational changes to evolve. Due to the financial and political power of the current educational system, most educational institutions will not welcome them. However, early signs are promising. For example, in 2012, the videos and programs of Khan Academy (http://www.khanacademy.org/) are used in over 10,000 classrooms. They represent the first level of digital teaching tools, using free videos. The next levels will be more sophisticated.

So, WIC is changing our societies from being brain-centric to being network centric; virtual applications will change daily life; knowledge work will require a change from traditional economics to value creation; manipulation of genes will change plants and animals; and tinkering with human biological matter might produce people with superhuman qualities.

Democratic governments will likewise face big challenges. Structural changes will involve a re-organization of citizen representation. To truly represent a community, an elected official will need constant district polls to measure the wishes of the people. But then the question arises: "Do future societies need representative government at all?" Couldn't internet polling be done at each level of government—town, district, county, state, and national? A citizen might register to vote for individual legislative issues at any of these levels. Already, people can sign online petitions quickly and easily, marking the introduction of a new democratic system. Of course, it gives a stronger voice to those citizens and residents who are interested in government affairs and want their beliefs promulgated and implemented. Managing one's knowledge capital will mean spending time and effort on politics and conflicts among belief systems.

Such demographic practices (online voting and discussion of issues) will become part of most communities, from corporations to sports clubs to cultural associations. Unlike traditional clubs, where one applied for membership and went to occasional club meetings or activities when convenient, the WIC community involves active, continuous information exchanges. The more an organization can keep the interest of its members, the healthier the community will be. It is difficult to forecast how long it will take until such systems are in place: A few years? Decades? Certainly, one can anticipate that leaders and beneficiaries of the old systems will resist such changes.

Will the biggest structural change do away with the nation-state? A nation-state used to be a community of a specific ethnicity whose members shared belief systems and values. It focused on the defense of the national community and its interests. Ethnic purity is disappearing in many countries, including the United States, West European countries, and even in the wealthier and more open countries of the Middle East, such as the United Arabic Emirates and Kuwait. WIC enables many companies to conduct business internationally, and trading is truly global. Virtual communities have begun to replace traditional communities, bringing together those with similar values and interests. At the same time, citizens around the world are dissatisfied with their governments, because they feel powerless and ignored. In many countries, immigration has changed any original cultural coherence. In the United States, many states and regions include differing belief systems and cultures. Other nations have been forcefully cobbled together through wars and power actions, with some sections wanting to separate from their nation-states. Even within the United States, some states have raised the possibility of seceding.

Can we imagine a system where a person can become a citizen of a virtual country that provides benefits and belief systems one prefers? Can a person live in New York, but feel more at home with those in Texas or California, for example, while another person who lives in Texas is culturally more at home with those in Boston? Communication capabilities today do not require preferences to be anchored in geography. With global business, travel, and workers routinely moving across borders, WIC may lead to a fresh look at whether historical national structures and nation-to-nation interaction will continue to be valid. Must we continue to plan the defense of our nation against another? Or will future wars be conducted against groups within nations? The war against terrorism illustrates the point. Terrorists are members of a belief system that thinks it can only influence other belief systems with violence. The September 11 attack was conducted by Saudi Arabian nationals, yet the United States has close friendly relationships with Saudi Arabia. The war in Afghanistan is not against the country, but against an internal community with a combative belief system (the Taliban). I predict that within the next twenty or thirty years, the first attempts will be made to dissolve national systems in favor of information community systems.

As for the modern economy, productivity and economic well-being currently depend on enticing consumers to buy more and newer goods. But before anything is produced, the need or desire for it needs to be measured. Now, Google and others implement search engines that "read people's minds" through their internet activity and identify interests and potential product needs. New advertising methods both respond to and stimulate such systems. This structural change from general public advertising to targeting just those who are interested is dramatic. If someone mentions golf in an internet message, an ad may immediately pop up for golf equipment or golf balls. Some people consider this function a violation of their privacy, while others find it useful. These economic changes are evolving as the world of mobile digital companions combines location interests with other information resources. As a result, traditional advertising will decline and people will lose jobs, but new opportunities will arise. Sales functions and targeted advertising will be integrated into new ways of doing business.

What about the world of science? Will scientific research expand because of WIC? Surely, DNA research couldn't have been done without tremendous computing power. Other fields, too, have expanded knowledge through advanced computation. Ian Foster cites the profound impact on "astrophysics (modeling, for example, mechanism for supernova explosions), climate (understanding global change), astronomy (digital sky surveys), and genetics (sequencing genomes)".[91] He alleges that in every scholarly discipline, "the future impact seems certain to be greater." There will be increased understanding of entire systems in addition to individual breakthroughs. This is in line with the history of invention: outsiders of the science establishment may pose the new idea or question. The establishment will then test its validity. This brings two points to mind. First, there will be more people within WIC who raise new ideas and ask questions outside the belief system of a scientific specialty. Second, in a restructured information community, their voices will have a better chance to be heard.

While systematic and structural changes that may result from WIC seem obvious, it is more difficult to predict personal changes because of a conflict of forces. Systems and structural changes can follow a trend led by better communication and efficiency. But when it comes to changes in our personal lives, the issues are more complex. With more knowledge and information available to most people, will it be used for a better world? Herein lies the difficulty, because the term "better world" may mean completely different things to different people. One person might think a better world is one in which her standard of living is higher. Another might prefer a world that is sustainable—not threatened by lack of resources, global warming, a shortage of food, and so on. Others consider a better world to be one where wars and violence are banned, or where minimum living standards are established worldwide. While WIC

---

91   Ian Foster, "How Computation Changed Research," *Switching Codes: Thinking Through Digital Technology in the Humanities and Arts,* ed. Thomas Bartscherer and Roderic Coover (Chicago: University of Chicago Press, Kindle Edition, 2011), location 175.

presents a different social model, it most likely will not automatically provide better conditions for everyone. It may even create conditions that are worse for some. The challenge is to understand the new conditions and to react to them. A plant or animal has to react to environmental conditions. There is a ray of hope that rationality may increase on this planet and that better ideas will take hold in our societies. Can more knowledge and an increase in rational thinking bring better behavior and less violence? The possibility exists, but time will tell whether we can actualize it.

We know that the value of information accessing and processing will increase. In real terms, this means that:

- People must seek a better understanding and management of their knowledge capabilities. This includes an understanding of one's personal knowledge acquisition history (the autobiography of knowledge described earlier), as well as awareness of knowledge one may have rejected. The result is a better understanding of one's intelligence systems.
- Identification and management of emotional motivators is very important for personal knowledge capital. Understanding when emotional motivators can drive us to specific actions is useful. Future digital companions may identify stimuli that prompt anger (or fear, or vengefulness, and so on), alerting the person or a counselor and suggesting alternatives or management techniques.

Will the society of the late twenty-first century uphold the notion that moments of irrational information processing should be punished with incarceration? Or will forms of punishment and treatment based on managing human information processing become acceptable? In time, digital companions may sense a person's emotions and artificially redirect reactions. If this sounds outrageous, remember that decades ago, anyone with severe behavioral health issues was considered dangerous and was locked up in an institution, segregated from society. Today, many people with mental health issues are integrated into communities, sometimes in supervised community living. Could the same be considered for those whose information processing temporarily goes wrong? Chemical influence can be a major impediment to personal information processing. People under the influence of alcohol, drugs or other chemicals may decide and act irresponsibly. There are signs that our society may use sensors to control such behavior. For instance, the automotive industry is working on sensors that detect when a driver is drowsy or when reaction time slows. Will similar sensors be used at home or in bars? Already, technologies that sense many health indicators are being developed. Nonintrusive sensing devices may identify the impact of chemical influences on the brain around the clock to improve behavioral health and prevent unwanted behavior.

What about the relationship between human thinking and digital information processing as knowledge and information shift from being brain-centric to WIC-centric? Imagine computers becoming more powerful both in memory and information processing. Could they become a competitor to human thinking, or even a dominating, restrictive force? Will our lives be guided in key aspects by a "master computer" the same way that GPS navigation tells us where to go? It is more likely that, just as with GPS, we will continue to choose our own goals and that future apps will help us find the best way to achieve them. But the biological brain is less than perfect. Emotional motivators influence the brain's algorithms, interfering with logical deduction and reasoning. Memory is flawed; belief systems greatly determine the patterns we recognize. We see or hear what we want to see or hear.

Several fundamental changes will affect the future of information in our society. Just as manipulations of physical substances led to modern natural sciences, manipulation of living beings, including human ones, is becoming part of the information society. Through elective surgery, parents can shape their children, body parts can be transplanted, and genes manipulated. Will this tinkering with the traditional human lead to radical changes in the next century or two? Is the vision of the posthuman society to be taken seriously—that is, will the content of our minds be transferred to a digital database, offering the option to live on in a virtual life once the biological body has decayed?

Is this monstrous new information network going to outmaneuver people? Could it assemble sufficient knowledge to live as the first technical-digital being that learns how to find fuel (build, maintain, and manage the devices that create energy to sustain it), protect itself against enemies, and ensure its future when parts fail? If possible at all, is such a scenario decades or hundreds of years out?

In the meantime, we have to learn how to live in this new information environment. We have to learn to take advantage of the accessibility of information that can create a path toward a better world. However, it comes with negative effects such as loss of privacy and (most painfully, at least in the short term) a shift in employment.

What is the role of people if, in a few centuries time, computers or robots have also replaced their jobs? There are no clear answers, but I believe that there will be a shift from measuring production to measuring value. This value will be expressed in ideas and research, in creativity that we have shown, for example, in developing these technologies and that we show each night when our minds take a few data points and assemble complete, detailed stories: our dreams. No computer could easily do this. However, to succeed, we must learn to value information and knowledge and treat it as our most valuable capital next to our health.

New Values for Information?

It is my dream that humans will enter a new stage—in which they depart somewhat from evolutionary emotional drivers and reduce unethical and emotional behavior. Violence could be reduced, animosity diminished, and machines could produce and manage other machines that then produce food, houses, and daily necessities. What, then, will be our role? Research, art, and designing better ways of living could be central challenges for us.

WIC enables us to use information differently. It is not good or evil; it is a new tool for intelligent life. People can use it to make the world better, or they can oppress others with intentional misinterpretation and disinformation. A first step toward managing WIC well would be to consider major goals for the world community in the twenty-first century. I challenge the reader to help create value in some form, such as apps and information systems that encourage and teach people, to achieve the following:

1. Making this planet sustainable: addressing the threats of climate change, reducing reliance on fossil fuel, and managing the global ecosystem (including plant and animal preservation, improving soil and water conditions, and environmentally friendly land use).

2. Providing intellectual assistance to establish minimum living conditions for all people on the planet, focusing on sufficient food, shelter, healthcare, entertainment, and the provision of knowledge capital.

3. Enabling transparency and fairness in all governments, promoting equality among all people, and providing free access to knowledge.

4. Controlling and reducing violence, an animalistic trait that does not fit into the new era of knowledge. The new WIC era will provide the basis for its reduction or elimination.

5. Acquisition of knowledge as the trademark of the human race in the twenty-first century. People should be encouraged to question, to seek to know more, to identify their own knowledge capital, and to amass more knowledge capital for value creation.

6. The opportunity for "reasonable happiness" for everyone in the information/knowledge age. "Happiness" is a vague term with no single, agreed-upon definition. In the United States, it may connote personal wealth creation, while in some European countries, it is about social justice and safety nets. Happiness is so difficult to define that researchers tend to use the term "well-being." Scales that attempt to measure well-being show substantial differences among countries. Perhaps in a few decades, politicians will campaign with objectives for well-being.

These goals will take time to achieve, but healthy discussion may lead us a few steps toward them. The move from a production-based economy to an information-based economy is significant. In many ways, we need to rethink society's objectives, and change them from maximum production and the encouragement of maximum consumption to value creation.

History shows that when more information is made available to large groups of people, societies advance. For example, in the Age of Enlightenment, more information led to democracy and a focus on art and freedom. The move toward equality and freedom are a recurring theme in human development. Signs indicate that the Arab Spring and the Occupy Wall Street movement have been enabled by information technology as they strive for governmental and organizational transparency, as well as greater freedom and fairness for all.

The Grand View

This book has described how humans made the big leap forward from intelligence at the first level (maximizing brain functions and memory) to the second level (supplementing the brain's memory with aids such as books), allowing culture and civilization to thrive. The third level of intelligence, which is just beginning, moves from brain-centric to WIC-centric intelligence. People are at a crossroads as WIC offers the potential of a more rational approach. This move to digital transparency, fairness, and democracy could give people a more direct voice in government and could overcome knowledge gaps through creative digital learning tools.

Religion could also be affected. In the first level of intelligence, people moved from multiple gods to one all-encompassing and exclusive god. The second level has been firmly based on competing religions that each serve a god. The third level offers the opportunity to focus on the commonalities of religions, find ways to cooperate, and merge their traditions into a vision of a god who can provide hope and support for all people. It is hoped that religious conflicts will soon become a thing of the past.

As researchers find out more about life, they may discover an artificial way to transition from the inorganic state to life. This will be just the beginning of understanding how life started on this planet, and the big challenge will be to determine how the most basic biological being learned to find fuel, survive in the environment, and replicate. Life cannot survive without information processing and the most basic memory collection.

Developments in the first level of intelligence took more than five hundred thousand years, during which the brain continuously developed. The second level took just a few thousand years as people used information aids such as books to manage knowledge. From the early days of computer processing, it took only a few decades to reach the third level: WIC, the new era of intelligence. WIC has created the new platform on which the future of this planet will be built. We must become aware of the evolutionary changes it is stimulating and its demands on our lives. Knowledge acquisition and information management will be key elements. Above all, the management of knowledge capital will provide the opportunity for each of us to become more responsible and better participants in the planet's ecosystem, enhancing our future and that of our planet.

www.ingramcontent.com/pod-product-compliance
Lightning Source LLC
Chambersburg PA
CBHW051236050326
40689CB00007B/935